MW00426192

WHAT OTHERS SAY ABOUT HOSS

Wow! Hoss has created a masterpiece. *Listing Boss* is going to change a lot of businesses and lives. Read this book!
  Frank Klesitz/CEO, Vyral Marketing

Hoss' advice and expertise has guided me through the process of going from being a solo agent to having a team behind me. We'll sell over 200 homes this year. He knows what's working and what's not. He knows the difference between the shiny stuff and what's legit.
  Justin Woodall – Athens, GA

I needed someone who could take me to another level in my business, and I found him.
  Michelle Wauro – Scottsdale, AZ

I worked four days a week and made over $275,000 last year. I am very, very grateful for that. Hoss has challenged me to see a different perspective for my life in general, my business, and my family.
  Mike Koperna – Garnet Valley, PA

Hoss' training and tools are exceptional: the best pieces I've ever seen in the marketplace. I use the *Listing Boss* as a coaching/recruiting system. It's so powerful!
  Richard Moya – New Braunfels, TX

Hoss provides clearly defined, specific strategic plans on how to accomplish your goals in each area that you want to go after. Hoss doesn't specialize in one thing; he's been exemplary in many things: in many areas of marketing and sales.
  Sheila Fejeran – Dallas, TX

Hoss has provided me with phenomenal strategies, marketing tools, and valuable resources to grow my business. Based on everything that I have learned, these three POWERFUL words summarize my journey: CONFIDENT, CONSISTENT & CLARITY.
  Monica Benavides – Harlingen, TX

With Hoss giving me the guidance and information to push me forward, I've quadrupled my volume and gross commissions in one year.
Jeremy Qualley – West Fargo, ND

Thanks, Hoss, for getting me fired up and providing me with great resources in order to get my business on track. The systems you have provided me with have gotten me up to speed with technology in order to take my business to the next level.
Regina Drone – Kansas City, MO

With Hoss' help setting up my goals and my business plan, I have already had to go back and increase my income goals by well over $100,000.
Bo Winn – Raleigh, NC

After working the *Listing Boss* program, I was tearing it up in my market immediately. I listed four houses that first week I implemented his approach, and have sold all my listings in less than one month on the market. His systems work...I am living proof. I recommend him to anyone, except my competition!
Drew Langhart – Baton Rouge, LA

I think your *Listing Boss* is genius. It is really perking up the ears of a lot of sellers. I'm sleeping well at night knowing that I know exactly how to grow my business.
Kaley Shorter – Gainesville, FL

I have been licensed for six weeks and already have listed seven homes with your program totaling over $3.5 million in gross value. I hope no one else in Vancouver is on your program, because I'm going to take over this city!
Bill Laidler – Vancouver, BC

As agents, we are constantly bombarded by so-called gurus who have all the answers on how to get business easy. Hoss was 100% different. His approach is no nonsense and focuses on doing the critical activities that get you both now business and consistent business. I would have crawled over broken glass to have Hoss' system when I was a new agent.
Brad Brinkman – San Diego, CA

Just wanted you to know that the *Listing Boss* has been the greatest asset to the growth of my business. It's given me an increase in confidence and reduced the anxiety in picking up the phone to make those calls. I consistently ask myself, "Is what I'm doing a money making activity?"

Christopher McQueen – San Antonio, TX

When I am feeling burned out from prospecting or want fresh ideas and reminders of stuff that works, I reference *Listing Boss*.

Erik Barthel – St. Louis, MO

Listing Boss is phenomenal. It is the one-stop shop that can turn your business from the red to the green. If you are serious about your business, you will be serious about *Listing Boss*.

Jim Slack – Houston, TX

Listing Boss is a miracle for me. This training is a million times better than the competition. You are the BEST!

Penny Shenk – Marlton, NJ

Does *Listing Boss* work? Holy cow, it does! As agents, we get side-tracked with a whole bunch of other coaches, techniques, or better ways. *Listing Boss* gives hands-on tools to use; all we have to do is personalize it and go.

Rick Baker – Loveland, CO

Listing Boss ROCKS! I'm making more appointments now than I ever have in a short period of time. You've taught me to be a lot more direct, have my alter ego, and no longer be linear.

Rob Wiley – Sacramento, CA

Ever since *Listing Boss,* my business has reenergized itself like drinking a can of Red Bull. Hoss lays it out in a way that is easy to implement, and gets you going right away to start gaining momentum. I have tried other programs in the past, but there was no road map or blueprint like this. If your business is stuck in the muck, change your tires and put this system on auto drive.

Scott Williams – Detroit, MI

Listing Boss can really get you to change your mindset and show you how to market yourself. I found Hoss through a referral, and since then my business is far better.

Oliver Thompson, Zurich Manhattan Financial

Hoss' entire system is AWESOME! Hoss has transformed my business to a new level. The *Listing Boss* has streamlined my business and allows me to completely focus on taking listings (which is what I have been searching for). I have learned more with Hoss in two months than I learned in two years with other coaches and trainers!

Mike Porciau – Austin, TX

Like taking candy from a baby. Today I had 33 attempts, spoke with eight leads, and made four appointments. Plus, I have four others that are very close to meeting with me. That was just after one hour of prospecting.

Connie Carlson – Atlanta, GA

Hoss has a very inspirational way of helping others realize the goals they need to set and meet. I knew he was extremely good at what he does as soon as our class started. He had us dial a FSBO and put them on speakerphone while we all listened silently. He converted the seller to an appointment within minutes. He then handed out the appointment to one of the agents in his class. Everything we learned made sense, and it seemed as though anyone can implement his systems effortlessly and produce business.

Naseem El-Barbarawi – Chicago, IL

Hoss Pratt is a great presenter, trainer, coach, and his systems are outstanding. He is a true master.

Luka Popovich – Chicago, IL

I just wanted to take a minute to tell you how grateful I am. You have no idea how many years I've spent wishing for this kind of training. I know it's going to change my business. Thanks so much for all you do. I really appreciate you.

Jami Church – Wichita, KS

You've taught me to step out of my boundaries, taught me to have faith in myself, reminded me that there is more to having just a work-geared mind, and the importance of focusing on other things than just business. You've illustrated the importance of focusing on me every once in a while (what a concept), and most importantly you've guided me to the net that appears and will EVERY TIME when I make any kind of jump in life.
Chelsea Countryman – Alamogordo, NM

Hoss' systems are so specific, thorough, and step-by-step that it makes it easy to implement as well as extremely effective. In my first year in the business I produced $12 million in sales volume from following his models and coaching.
Brandon Browning – Baton Rouge, LA

The passion that Hoss puts into the content he creates for everyone is astonishing. I can't speak highly enough about what Hoss has given me and the value he brings. I recommend him without reservation.
Darren James – Baton Rouge, LA

Hoss Pratt always has a forward approach to everything. He's taught me many lessons and provided many tools that have been instrumental in growing my real estate business.
Dave Pannell – Ft. Worth, TX

Things have really changed in marketing over the last 30 years. The information I've learned from Hoss has blown me away, and has allowed me the ability to stay ahead of the curve in many areas.
Jaymes Willoughby – Austin, TX

Like most agents, we struggled to find more buyers and sellers; that was until we discovered Hoss. Within six months following his models and coaching we have doubled our business and we plan to do that again this year.
Eleanor & Maurice King – Brooklin, ON

LISTING
BOSS

The Definitive Blueprint for Real Estate Success

HOSS PRATT

Clovercroft Publishing

Listing Boss: The Definitive Blueprint for Real Estate Success

©2017 by Hoss Pratt

Published by Clovercroft Publishing, Franklin, Tennessee.

Cover Design by Roberto Secades

Interior Design by Suzanne Lawing

Edited by Tawnya Austin

Printed in the United States of America

978-1-945507-35-9

DEDICATION

*First, to my family for always loving and
supporting me on my journey.*

*Second, to my mentors who have poured your wisdom into me;
I wouldn't be where I am without your guidance.*

*Third, to my Tribe for listening to me
and allowing me to do what I do.*

*Fourth, to all the seekers...
may you find much more than you're looking for in this book and in life.*

CONTENTS

INTRODUCTION

A friend recently asked me, "Hoss, what is the real reason for writing this book?" While I will get into many specifics in the pages to follow, the simple answer is *to inspire and equip you to live your dream.* I want to help guide you from living ordinary to living *legendary.*

If you're looking for a magic pill, you've come to the wrong place. There are a lot of people who will sell it to you, but I know that for you to be more valuable and to have more, you will have to work for it. What you will get is a solid foundation and 12 essential philosophies to create real estate success, dominate your market, and make your competition irrelevant.

> DON'T LIVE ORDINARY ... LIVE LEGENDARY.

In these pages, I will challenge you to take control of your own destiny and give you the tools to do so. I will help you clarify your vision and share concepts and systems that will give you no choice but to create success. I will help you remove all the excuses you have for not achieving extraordinary success and show you simple ways to set yourself up to truly live the life of your dreams. An unidentified student of Warren G. Tracy said, "You have to be willing to spend a few years of your life like most people won't so you can spend the rest of your life living like most people can't."

I've identified three distinct success factors for living the life of your dreams. The first is Mindset. I've devoted an entire chapter of this book to helping you change your mindset to be prepared for doing the things to get the results you want. How you think can make or break your ability to achieve your goals and dreams.

The second factor for living your dream life is having proven business Models. Every person needs to have models to follow: role models, processes, systems, scripts, books, videos, and more. Consider this book your model. It's a model; however, you've got to do your part, which leads me to the third factor.

The third factor for extraordinary success is to take Massive Action. Notice I didn't just say you have to take action; you have to take massive action. Everybody takes action, right? This is the part that's up to you. Know that if you apply massive action to the principles and the 12 essential philosophies I have laid out in this book, you'll absolutely live your dream and be able to achieve the results that you want—and achieve them consistently.

CHANGE YOUR MINDSET

Perhaps the most critical thing that will impact your success is having the right mindset. Part of that mindset is your willingness to change. Change can be scary, and it can be painful. Change can also open up your world to new opportunities that you had only previously imagined. I've learned from coaching others in this business that what they are thinking now got them where they are. To get you to a new level, I've got to get you to change your thinking. To be successful, that's what I had to do personally.

As a young entrepreneur in my teens, I had a successful lawn service business, but I didn't feel like I was using my full potential. I felt stuck. I wasn't sure what to do, but I was fortunate enough to have a mentor who took me under his wing and helped me make the best decision of my life—to get into the real estate business. As part of his advice, it required me to uproot from my home in northwest Missouri. I remember that conversation like it was yesterday. Jimbo said, "Hoss, you've got to move to Dallas." I asked him, "Why do I have to move to Dallas?" His answer was, "Because you belong there. You can make a hundred thousand dollars a year here, or you can make a million dollars a year there." He had my attention.

I had never been on an airplane before, but he said, "Let's go to Dallas and check it out." So we went to Dallas. We drove around, and I saw the opportunity and determined I wanted to live there. To assure that I would follow through, he had me choose a date right then when

I would move. The date would be November 15. On November 15 at 2:30 in the morning, I loaded up my truck with my TV and my suitcase, and I drove southbound on Interstate 35 toward Dallas. I never looked back, because I was here to build my business and (more importantly) my dream life.

I got my real estate license, and I got active. My first six months was brutal. I sold a lot of things to survive, but no real estate. I blew $50,000 trying everything, taking action, and finding out what did and did not work. In fact, I should do a whole book on what not to spend your money on to be successful. There were a lot of lessons learned. Then I had an epiphany. I discovered what I'm going to share with you in this book. I learned strategies, methods, and ideas. I changed my thinking in a way that changed everything for me. If I had not been willing to change, I was going to be out of business. In getting to the next level, I had to manage my fear or let it win.

It was around this time that I listened to my first Jim Rohn recording. He said something that had a profound impact on me, and I've designed my whole life around the concept. Here's what he said:

If you will change, everything will change for you. Don't wait for things to change. Change doesn't start out there; change starts within ... all change starts with you.

I learned that if I wanted a different outcome six months from now, a year from now, or five years from now, the only thing I had to worry about was me. Go to work on me. Change me. I looked in the mirror and said, "You are the reason you don't have the results you want right now. What are you going to do about it?"

As a result of my epiphany and subsequent changes, 30 days later I had 30 listings. My very first year, I achieved rookie of the year. All those results came in the second part of my first year, and all because I changed my mindset and implemented the things I'm going to share with you in this book. That's how fast you can obtain results by simply changing your mindset.

UTILIZE MODELS

Let me tell you what this book is not about. It is not about becoming a better real estate agent; it's about becoming a better businessperson. Think about your market. Most agents run this business like a hobby versus a business. They sell an average of four homes a year. They throw spaghetti at the wall to see what sticks. No thanks!

In this book, I will

- Take the guesswork out of the game for you by providing you with proven business models that will be game changers for your success. These models will include creating a marketing arsenal that will help you have a clear understanding of why someone should choose you over another agent.

- Include processes and systems that will support developing the right habits to reach your goals.

- Share with you ways to maximize your time and effort and identify your niche market so your efforts will be more focused.

- Show you how to focus on lead conversion and provide systems to manage the process.

- Coach you on how to master your listing presentations and the key elements for achieving your desired results.

- Guide you through the process of building a winning team that is perfectly suited for you and your niche to maximize your effectiveness.

- Teach you techniques to practice the power of persuasion and influence to get people off the fence and take action.

There is no reason to reinvent the wheel when these models are proven. Some of them may even be things you already know about, but I can assure you that I will share with you how to execute them in such a way that you will differentiate yourself from your competition. All of this will support you in your journey to take your business to the next level, but it takes massive action on your part.

TAKE MASSIVE ACTION

You can have the best plans in the world and get no results if you don't take action. It is amazing to me how many people fall short on execution when they have all the tools in front of them to be successful.

What does it mean to take massive action? It means committing to the process, every day, every hour, every minute. It means doing things that others are not willing to do so you can be your best you. It means leaving all the excuses behind. The key philosophies in this book make up your blueprint. If you do the work, you will get the results. It is time to own your success.

DISCIPLINE IS THE GATEKEEPER OF SUCCESS.

This book was written for you. It was written for you to be the model that you, too, can follow to achieve extraordinary results in your real estate business. I built an extremely successful multi-million-dollar real estate business and sold it. Today I have taken my learning and I teach, coach, and train agents all over the country. In fact, I've conducted over 1,300 seminars in 48 states. I've shared over 1,400 online webinars and events. I've knocked on over 100,000 doors. I've made over 200,000 prospecting calls. I have over 5,500 one-on-one hours of coaching top agents around the country. I've learned a lot about how to get an agent from stuck to unstuck and how they get to the next level in their business. Will it be easy? No. Will it be worth it? Yes.

Here is my commitment to you: if you will be disciplined in following these steps, you will create unbelievable success. Discipline is the gatekeeper of success. There are a lot of people who are not willing to do what it takes to succeed. Succeeding is tough. Being successful, having continuous growth, and achieving your goals are hard. The marketplace will make you earn success. However, when you have the right mindset, when you utilize the most innovative marketing tools, when you put the most efficient systems in place, and when you understand what needs to be done to get the most conversion opportunities, it becomes a lot easier. I'm excited to take you on this transformational journey. Let's begin.

1. Create a Vision

If you are working on something exciting that you really care about,
you don't have to be pushed. The vision pulls you.
—Steve Jobs

To create a true transformation in your life, you have to get serious about knowing where you're going and be willing to do the things that will get you there. What's important to you?

I have found in my own life that vision is a tremendous motivator. I have also been amazed at the number of people I have met over the years who are some of the hardest working people I have ever met, yet they don't achieve their desired level of success because they don't know what it is they are working towards. They don't know where they are going, so how can they reach their destination?

Think about it. Some of the world's biggest success stories started with leaders who had a great vision and then put a plan in action to achieve success. Possibly one of the biggest visionaries of all time was Henry Ford. He became famous for changing the face of the auto industry with the revolutionary idea of using an assembly line to mass-produce automobiles. He did this by raising funds from friends and negotiating deals with potential vendors and suppliers that gave him credit because they believed in the vision.

A more modern-day example of someone with extraordinary vision is Sam Walton. He had a vision, a radical vision, to deliver cost-cutting products to the retail industry. Possibly the biggest secret to Walmart's growth is that Walton was the first to employ a computer expert to develop the company's logistics and inventory systems, which created unparalleled efficiencies and enabled Walmart to compete at a level better than virtually every other retail and department store in existence.

I want to give you the tools to make sure you know what your vision and goals are and put systems in place to help you accomplish them beyond your wildest imagination. I want you to stretch yourself and have the courage and dedication to set yourself up for extraordinary success.

WHAT DOES SUCCESS LOOK LIKE?

Success means something different to every person. To you, success may be reaching a specific income, buying a new car, building a house, finding the perfect mate, or travelling the world. Every person is different, and success means something unique to each of you. Don't make the mistake of trying to be like someone else. This is *your* dream and *your* life. Design your life in a way that each day motivates you more than the last because you have everything you ever imagined.

THERE IS NOT A MORE POWERFUL MOTIVATOR THAN A CLEAR VISION.

So, let me ask you a question. What does your business and your life look like in 5 years, 10 years, 20 years? Where do you live? What subdivision? What neighborhood? Be specific. I'm living in the house I knew I was going to live in three years before I completed the purchase. What kind of car do you drive? What about your family? Do you have any new family members? How much money do you have? How much money do you have saved up? How much money do you give away? What about your health? Do you feel good? Do you look good? Picture your life five years from now and visualize it. What is important to you? What does this picture look like in order for you to feel successful?

This picture, this vision, represents why you're doing what you're doing. This is why you get out of bed every day, so you want to be able to see it, smell it, touch it, taste it. You want it to be so clear that it's not a vision to you; it's totally reality. It's going to happen. This is going to be your fuel every single day.

Let me also give you a little piece of advice when creating your vision. Don't get too stuck on thinking you have to have all the answers right now. In the words of the great Zig Ziglar, "Go as far as you can see; when you get there, you'll be able to see farther." Create a picture of the life you want.

On days when you don't feel like lead generating, the vision will carry you. It is a reminder that it's not about you. It's about your vision. You've got to fulfill that vision. It's not about your thoughts and your feelings right now. It's about the vision. Do you know the reason I've never missed a day of lead generation in my life, ever, besides the fact that I grew up working on a farm, and I have an extreme work ethic? The reason is I've always had a vision. I've always known where I was going to go. There is not a more powerful motivator than a clear vision.

FOCUS ON YOUR VISION

There's a thing called definiteness of purpose. It is spoken of in one of the best books that I've ever read, which is Napoleon Hills' *Think and Grow Rich*. In sharing his 17 Principles of Personal Achievement, it is lesson number one. Definiteness of purpose is the starting point of all achievement. Without a purpose and a plan (a vision), people drift aimlessly through life. When you have a vision and your focused action is on that vision, there's a power behind it. Fortune favors those bold enough to move beyond their fear and step out before they have all the answers. The answers will come to you. Be comfortable with just taking action and having faith that you're on the right path because you have the definiteness of purpose. Follow your life's purpose without questioning why. Keep moving forward, and here's what will happen … the right people will come into your life at the right time. Be fearless in this pursuit. Don't second-guess yourself. Just do it.

I'm living the life today that I envisioned many years ago because I focused on my vision. That's what I want for you. I want you to start living life for the vision instead of the present. Many people say to live life in the present. It is true that you should enjoy the present moment, of course. But don't let your emotions and your fears for right now determine your future. Always keep your eyes down the road on where you're going because when you're looking down the road, and you see where you're going, that's what it's all about. Nothing else matters.

Let me give you a visual example. When I was a junior in high school, I started a lawn service. I grew the business and mowed 80 lawns a week. I had all my best friends working for me. I went out and got a loan at 17, and I bought a lot of really nice commercial equipment because I knew that to do the job at the level that was needed, I needed to be 100% committed to the quality of the work. I also needed to equip those working for me to do the job right.

In Missouri, the grass lays down in a way that it looks like a base-ball field, so it is common to mow diamonds in it. Mowing grass there is almost like artwork. When you have this expensive commercial equipment, it leaves very defined lines and, if the lines are crooked, the yard will look like a mess even if it mowed evenly. When I would train my mowers, I would always tell them, "You don't look at any-thing but a focal point." To keep a straight line, all you have to do is find a focal point.

Why have a focal point? Because a focal point tells you where you're going. Without it, that straight line will look like a zigzag or just a crooked mess. Don't take your eyes off of the focal point and move to-wards it. In this case, don't look anywhere—down, up, left, right—but straight ahead toward the focal point. Your focal point is your vision. Don't look down, don't look up, and don't look sideways. Go straight towards your focal point, and you will create a beautiful masterpiece called the life of your dreams.

THINK BIGGER

What I want you to do now is think about your goals, but I want you to think bigger than you've ever thought before. Why? Because you can't live an extraordinary life by thinking small. Remember those visionaries we talked about earlier? Could they have achieved the same level of success by thinking small, or even thinking ordinary? My experience in working with thousands of agents over the last 10 years is that getting people to bust through their preconceived notions about what is possible and truly identify the things they are passionate about and focus on those passions and where they're going, that they are able to accomplish more than they ever believed was possible. I want that for you. More importantly, *you* should want that for you. What would your life look like if you removed all the limits?

I recently met a man who is rapidly becoming one of the country's most sought-after speakers. His name is Nick Vujicic, and he was born with no arms and no legs. He is a best-selling author of several books, and he speaks all over the world about living a rich, fulfilled life by finding your purpose despite what difficulties you believe are in the way. He lives independently and has a beautiful wife and two boys. He swims, plays soccer, and has impacted millions all over the world because he determined at a young age, along with encouragement from his parents, that he would look past what the world perceived as his disabilities. He is truly leading the life of his dreams—with no limits.

How do you get there? First, you have to ask yourself some questions, and you need to be honest about the answers. There is no right and wrong here. This is about you and your life. This is about what you want for your future. It isn't about anybody else. If you've never done this exercise before, it may take some time to think through everything you really want.

WHAT ARE YOUR GOALS?

Get out a single sheet of paper. You may have to edit the sheet a few times, and that's okay. Your goals are a living, breathing, and ever-changing thing. As you accomplish one thing, something else will take its place as a new goal. There are even times when something that was important to you before is no longer a priority, so you will remove it. The key is to have a focal point for where you are going. Having your goals on a single sheet of paper is important because I want you to read it every day, and if it isn't concise and easy to read, chances are you won't be committed to following the process. Making it simple makes it doable. And if you don't stay focused on your goals, chances are high you won't achieve them. Having your goals on one page will give you a simple visual roadmap to follow.

> SUCCESS WITHOUT FULFILLMENT IS THE ULTIMATE FAILURE.
>
> –TONY ROBBINS

When you think about your goals, I don't want you to just think about your real estate goals. After all, real estate is not your life; it's your occupation, right? It is only one part of who you are. It's a vehicle that we chose to fulfill our vision.

I'm continually amazed at how many real estate agents fly by the seat of their pants, have created nothing that makes them unique, and have no vision, no goals, and no system for success. And they wonder why they're broke. Yet this is how many agents operate. You won't be successful, however, without a plan to get there. So let's talk about goals. Building the life that you want commands looking at nine key elements and defining the goals you want in each element. These elements are

1. Business
2. Physical health
3. Spiritual
4. Educational
5. Family/Relationships
6. Personal
7. Financial
8. Lifestyle
9. Mental/Attitude

Let me tell you a funny story. When I first got into real estate, I had a mentor who showed me the ropes and helped me learn how to become successful. He was talking to me one day after I first moved to Dallas, and he told me I needed to set some goals. I remember I was sitting in my two-bedroom apartment, and I spent all night seriously thinking about and setting my goals. I was about 21 years old at the time—young and confident (or cocky) enough to think I was going to take over the world. I was going to dominate the market. I was going to just be stupid rich by the time I was 25, sell a million homes, and own many real estate offices.

I set these goals because I always thought big. We should think big, right? I always thought huge, and that's probably why growing up in northwest Missouri working on a farm didn't suit me very well, because I thought bigger than that. But here's what he did. I sent my mentor the goals I created, and he sends me back an email with a one sentence reply. It said, "The Brinks truck doesn't follow the hearse."

That's all he said, and I felt really stupid. What did that mean? What he meant was that I could make all the money in the world, but when I left this world I couldn't take it with me, and what I needed to do was build a life and not just build wealth.

Once the light bulb came on, he said to me, "Hoss, you can't just go after all the money and success in the world and expect to be fulfilled," and he was so right.

Since that conversation, I've met many successful people. I'm talking highly successful real estate agents, brokers, business people, and entrepreneurs, and there are a lot of them who are totally unfulfilled. So what is it that

THE MORE SPECIFIC YOU MAKE YOUR GOALS, THE MORE SPECIFIC YOU WILL EXPERIENCE RESULTS.

would fulfill you? If you think building a fifty-million-dollar-a-year real estate team is going to fulfill you, you're confused. It's not going to happen. There are other areas in your life that you need to get fulfillment from in addition to the business side. I don't want you reach your business goals and in the process lose your family, your health, your kids, or have your friends turn their backs on you. I don't want that, and you don't want that. I want you to be fulfilled because that is where you will find true happiness. You need to get this piece right, because if you screw this part up, none of the rest of it will matter.

THE NINE AREAS OF A BALANCED, HAPPY LIFE

Let's break down the nine areas to create a balanced, happy life, and I want you to set goals for each area. If you already have goals, that's a great start. Chances are they are primarily focused on your business or financial goals. So humor me and let's walk through each of these elements and create some specific goals. These are in no particular order as far as importance—each one is important in its own way to creating your dream life. Remember, your goal is to become more valuable, and to become more valuable, you have to work on you. The fact that you're reading this book means you want to become more valuable, so let's get started in planning out the next year of your life.

Business. What are your business goals? Be very specific. How much do you want to grow? How many houses do you want to sell? What type of houses? Do you want to create a niche? Do you want to add other team members? What are the top 5–10 things you want to accomplish in your business in the next 12 months?

Physical Health. Most people don't think about how important their physical health is to achieving the other goals in their life. Sure, some people want to lose weight or work out more, but they rarely attribute good health to something that can significantly impact their ability to accomplish the other things in life they want. But think about it. Being successful takes a lot of energy and endurance. Having strong physical health is a great contributor to helping accomplish all the other elements of building a balanced life. Think about specific goals you have to obtain better physical health. Is it to lose a specific amount of weight? Is it to work out more? If so, what does that look like? How often do you want to go to the gym, and what do you want to accomplish while you're there? Maybe you want to run a marathon. It could be things you need to stop doing, like eating fast food or smoking. Maybe you want to recover from an injury. Whatever it is, write it down.

Spiritual. To have fulfillment, it is important to draw strength from a higher power. For me, my faith brings me inspiration and guidance that grounds me. I have very specific goals in this area as a leader for my family. Wherever you draw your spiritual strength from, set some specific goals that will support and inspire you. The more specific you make your goals, the more specific you will experience results.

Educational. Oftentimes, once we finish our formal education, we don't think of ourselves as needing continuing education on our journey. Nothing could be further from the truth. To be your best you and to continue to be more valuable, you need to grow your mind. How do you do that? One way is to read more. Do you have a goal to read a certain number of books this year? What type of books? What about seminars or courses that can help you grow? Do you have a personal coach? Is that something you should consider? How will you continue to educate yourself so you are growing?

Family/Relationships. Family/relationships are huge. What are your goals for your family? To me, family is the most important thing. One of my primary goals is to ensure the strength and vitality of my marriage. If you've ever heard me speak, you know I talk about my wife all the time. I know how blessed I am to have Mykanna, so I work on that relationship every day because I don't ever want to take her for granted. Who are the most important people in your life? What do you want to accomplish in these relationships? Do you want to take the kids to Disneyland? Is it a fishing trip with your dad? Are you keeping in touch with your parents and siblings like you want to? What does that look like? Who are the people that you want to know are important to you, and how do you plan to strengthen those relationships over the next year? What are you going to do? I also have a family goals board. In fact, my youngest daughter's first goal was to get potty trained.

Personal. You might think that all of these are personal, and they are in a way. But this is about doing something that is just for you. Maybe you want to learn to scuba dive or spend more time playing tennis. A couple of my personal goals are to learn how to play Texas hold 'em poker and play guitar. Maybe you want to learn to speak a new language or push yourself to do something you've never done before. Maybe you want to get more rest. What is it that you want to do that's just for you?

Financial. Your financial goals should not be just about creating revenue. This is your whole financial picture. Do you want to pay off debt? What debt, and how much? Maybe you want to put a certain amount of money in savings or in a retirement plan. Do you want to invest in a second home? Purchase some rental property? Do you want to start planning for your children's future with a college fund or a trust fund? What are your financial goals for the next year?

Lifestyle. What does lifestyle mean? This is a way of living expressed in activities, attitudes, interests, opinions, values, and allocation of time. Are there habits you want to break? Are there habits you want to create? Do you want to join a group or country club? What are your interests that you want to pursue more heavily? What do you need to improve or change to have the overall lifestyle you desire?

Mental/Attitude. The last one is mental attitude, and that's kind of a bonus element. In the next chapter we will talk more about mindset which is such a big piece to living a happy life. What attitudes do you need to change? How is your stress level? Do you need to incorporate things to remove unhealthy stress? Maybe you want to read inspirational messages to begin every day. Perhaps you need to eliminate negative people or things from your life. Maybe you want to have a time each day to quiet your mind through prayer or meditation or relaxation. Set some positive goals to relieve the pressure of the speed of life that will keep you mentally moving in the right direction.

Those are the nine elements needed to live a truly balanced life, and one that will lead to total fulfillment. Take each element seriously and really think through how you can utilize each to live your dream life. Create a goals sheet that looks something like the image on the next page.

GOALS

Business	Physical Health	Spiritual
_____	_____	_____
_____	_____	_____
_____	_____	_____
_____	_____	_____
_____	_____	_____
_____	_____	_____
_____	_____	_____

Educational	Family/Relationships	Personal
_____	_____	_____
_____	_____	_____
_____	_____	_____
_____	_____	_____
_____	_____	_____
_____	_____	_____
_____	_____	_____

Financial	Lifestyle	Mental/Attitude
_____	_____	_____
_____	_____	_____
_____	_____	_____
_____	_____	_____
_____	_____	_____
_____	_____	_____
_____	_____	_____

You can download this resource at www.listingboss.com/group

On your goals sheet I want you to write down 5-10 goals in each of these areas. I can't express enough to be specific. If you want to lose weight, write down how much. If you want to travel, be specific about where you want to go and what you want to see and experience. If you want to save more money, write down a specific amount and a date by when you want to achieve that amount. I want you to put some serious thought into this, and I want you to get this done this week. Start now and continue tweaking it until you have a balanced list. Go back over it and ask yourself how important each item is and make sure they contribute to achieving the vision you wrote down at the beginning of the chapter.

A great example of setting and achieving goals comes from the entertainment industry with actor Jim Carrey. Before Jim became a success, he had been in Hollywood for a long time, and he was broke and depressed. He drove up to Mulholland Drive every night in his beat-up Toyota, looked over the city, and daydreamed about his future success. He visualized specific things that he wanted. It made him feel better as he drove home to think about having those things, and while he didn't have them yet, he believed he would one day. On one of those nights in 1990, he did something extraordinary. Jim wrote himself a check for $10 million for "acting services rendered," and dated it for Thanksgiving 1995. He kept the check in his wallet and watched it deteriorate over the next five years. In the meantime, he had success with movies like *Ace Venture: Pet Detective*. Just before Thanksgiving 1995, he found out he got the lead part in *Dumb and Dumber*, and his salary for that movie would be $10 million. He went on to tell Oprah Winfrey during an interview in 1997, "I had an insane belief in my own ability to manifest things that I think is ultimately complete sanity. I believe we are creators, and we create with every thought and every word. I believe that every moment is pregnant with the next moment in your life."

I'll tell you again, today I'm living the life that I envisioned many years ago. I envisioned the qualities I would find in a wife. I definitely married up, but I envisioned it and knew what was important to me. It helped me become the person that woman would be attracted to, and it will help you get the things that you already deserve but don't know how to get for yourself. You have to envision it and set goals that will help you achieve your vision.

PLANT THE SEEDS

Now that you have your vision and your goals, you know where you're going. That's the starting point. But ... how do you get there? You have to start by planting the seeds that will make the vision grow. You do this by implementing habits that continue to make you better and grow who you are today into the person you need to be in order to achieve that vision and those goals.

> CREATING GOOD COMPOUNDING HABITS EXECUTED EVERY DAY IS THE KEY TO MAKING YOURSELF MORE VALUABLE AND ACHIEVING THE VISION YOU DESIRE.

In all my reading (and I read a lot), I follow a lot of trainers and speakers. Jim Rohn has had a huge impact on me, as well as Anthony Robbins. Imagine how many millions of lives those two people have changed, and Anthony Robbins was literally living in his car before he became successful. Jim Rohn says, "Every day you read, and every day you journal. Every day you do these things to become more valuable and becoming more valuable is the secret." So creating good compounding habits executed every day is the key to making yourself more valuable and achieving the vision that you desire.

It's not going to happen by just lying in bed until noon, right? Today is nothing but a result of your habits compounded over time. You have to plant the seeds to reap the harvest. That's all it is. The difference between somebody who's successful and someone who's not comes down to a choice. You become successful by making choices that support your success. You become more successful by the compounding effect of your daily choices, your daily habits. The best way to create good habits is to create a plan for your day, your week, and your month. What things do you need to intentionally make happen in order to achieve the things you said you wanted? I like to look at success as if the "rent is due every day."

For example, I believe getting up by six o'clock in the morning is a must. Statistics show that most millionaires and highly successful people start their day by six o'clock in the morning. It's called the Six O'Clock Club. Join it. One thing that every person has the same amount of as everyone else is time. We all have 24 hours each day, and while we may have different obligations, we have choices as to how we spend that time.

For me, I include 30-minutes of exercise every day. You've got to get exercise to give you the energy you need to execute all your goals and to be able to keep up with the fast pace of today's life. What are other ways to create strong habits? How often do you role-play and practice scripts? You've got to practice becoming better, and if you can become better over the phone and face-to-face, you will convert more leads and make more money. This is one of those things that is uncomfortable at first, and that is why so many people don't want to do it. It is also why so many people are bad at converting leads. They don't do the right things in the right way to get the results they want. Break out of your comfort zone and do things differently to get different results.

Here's a sample of what a week in real estate looked like for me. Yours may not look exactly like this, but you need to have a weekly goal. I call it the Weekly Goal Boss, and it serves as a tool to help make sure goals are turned into habits. This is an example of the extreme discipline it will take to get to the next level, and it won't happen without a plan because there are too many distractions that get in the way. You have to set yourself up to succeed. And to do that, you need to

Weekly Goal Boss Example

Action	Mon	Tues	Wed	Thur	Fri	Sat	Sun	Achieved	Goal	Net
6 O'Clock Club	X	X	X		X			4	6	-2
30 Min. Exercise	X	X		X	X			4	5	-1
Role Play Scripts	X		X		X			3	3	0
50 Prospecting Calls	X	X	X	X	X			5	5	0
1 Listing Presentation	X	X	X	X	X	X		6	3	3
5 Handwritten Notes	X	X		X				3	5	-2
Journal	X		X		X		X	4	7	-3
Read 10 Pages	X	X	X	X	X	X	X	7	7	0
Listen 30 Min. Audio	X	X	X	X	X	X		6	7	-1
Date Night w/Spouse			X			X		2	1	1
Pray/Meditate	X		X		X		X	4	7	-3
Time w/ Kids	X	X		X	X		X	5	4	1
Spend time at the Lake						X		1	1	0
							Total	54	61	-7

You can download this resource at www.listingboss.com/group

have a plan. Use the plan and track it. Customize it and own it. Track your success based on your level of execution and adjust accordingly.

Don't forget as a part of putting your goals into habits to read your vision and goals every single day. Know them inside and out so you build an intentional life.

There you have the foundation, the starting point. Pat yourself on the back for taking a critical step toward creating the life of your dreams. This is going to be fun, so enjoy the journey. In the chapters ahead, I will share with you the mindset, methods, tools, and proven processes to help you dominate your market.

☞ ACTIONS TO TAKE

1. Create your vision—what does the life of your dreams look like?
2. Write down your 5–10 goals in each of the nine key elements of your life.
3. Create your Weekly Goal Boss and track your results.
4. Journal every day.

♔ KEYS TO SUCCESS

1. There is not a more powerful motivator than a clear vision.
2. Go straight towards your focal point and you will create a beautiful masterpiece called the life of your dreams.
3. The more specific you make your goals, the more you will experience results.
4. Creating good compounding habits executed every day is the key to making yourself more valuable and achieving the vision that you desire.
5. Enjoy the journey.

2. Develop a Top-Producing Mindset

You have to change your thinking to change your results.
—Tony Jeary

I want to share with you where all this started on my journey, on why I'm even doing what I'm doing today. I come from a family of entrepreneurs that are extremely hard workers and focused on being successful. My dad has five brothers, and four out of the five are self-made millionaires. I watched each of them go from having virtually nothing to becoming millionaires, every one of them building their business on their own. The only exception was one uncle who went to college, and he became an attorney. Today he is one of the top trial attorneys in the country. None of the others attended college, so if that's an excuse you've used in the past for not becoming more successful, you need to throw it out the window today. One started a trucking company, another a computer company, and yet another a feed and farm/ranch store. Watching my uncles shattered so many beliefs for me and taught me so many different lessons.

Perhaps the most important lesson I learned from my uncles is that *the way you think* is an important part of succeeding. Even now, when I look at my life today, I am amazed at where I am. Don't we all want to be able to do what we want, when we want, with whom we want? I'm here to tell you that it's absolutely possible.

DESIRE & BELIEF

Desire is the beginning of the journey to do more, become more, and be the best you. Desire is the birthplace of motivation. That's the good news. The bad news is that desire alone won't make you successful. It takes your action to be able to make the desire come to fruition.

I believe it is likely that desire for success is the reason that you got into real estate. I remember telling my mentor, Jimbo, when I was 16 that I wanted to live a legendary life, and that I didn't want to let fear stop me. I remember having that conversation and the conviction of truly believing I could make it happen. Jimbo said, "Welcome to the club. That's the desire." Success starts with desire.

Everybody has potential and God-given talents and strengths. It's your job to find it and to cultivate that potential until it is fully bloomed. In real estate, if you take 100 agents from all over the country and follow those agents around to see what kind of results they get, here's what will happen. In a year, 1% of those 100 (that means only one agent) will have exponential increases; about 4% will have incremental increases; and 95% will do about the same amount of business or less. That's 95%. My desire for you is for you to be in that top 5% of agents that are always growing. It starts with the desire to be in that top-producing group. That's where freedom begins.

This industry has a revolving door. To stay in and thrive, you've got to change right now. Decide to embrace the change that you're about to go through because change is the only way you're going to be able to get the results—change the way you think and change what you're doing. Again, your actions for the last six months have gotten you today's result, and if you are unwilling to change, the next six months will be the same. Most people don't like change. Change can be scary because of all the unknowns, but you can let desire be stronger than your fear.

TWO KINDS OF MINDSETS

There is a great book called *Mindset* by Carol Dweck, a researcher for Stanford University, where she says there are two different types of mindsets. The first mindset is the fixed mindset. This person believes that their intelligence, personality, and character are inherent and static. They basically believe that their potential is determined at birth and that the way they live is their destiny—just the way it's supposed to be. They live their life going about trying to avoid failure and therefore don't change or improve. They prefer to look smart so they stick to what they know and avoid challenges. They're fixed.

On the other side of fixed is the growth mindset. This is the mindset that the most successful people adopt. This is the mindset of the top five-percenters. The growth mindset is the belief that your intelligence, personality, and character can be continuously developed and that your true potential is unknown and unknowable. In this mindset you realize you can make anything happen, and you can become anything you want to become without limitations. The growth mindset has the desire for continuous learning, to confront uncertainties, embrace challenges, and not be afraid to fail.

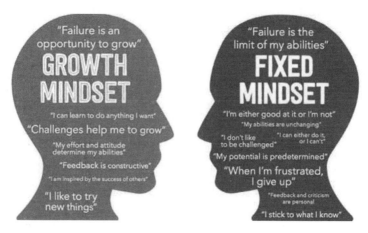

Which mindset do you have—fixed or growth? Which mindset do you want to have? I have the growth mindset; I always have. At times I may find myself doing a little fixed thinking, but I coach myself in that moment and remind myself I can make anything happen. This philosophy and this understanding is important. A lot of your family members, friends, and customers have a fixed mindset; you're not going to change them. As much as I want to change some people, I can't because they have a fixed mindset. Jimbo used to say, "You can't teach a pig to sing because it's really annoying to the pig, and it's a waste of your time." It's true. And that's okay, but you can choose growth over being static.

EVERYTHING YOU WANT IS ON THE OTHER SIDE OF FEAR.

I went from working on a dairy farm, barely making it through high school, from a rural area in Missouri, to living the life I have today. If I can do it, you can do it too, especially if you have the right tools that I had to discover on my own.

I don't just want you to change while the motivation is high. I want your change to be forever. I know that to change you forever, you've got to dig deep and be able to identify what you need to change.

FIVE WAYS TO DEVELOP A GROWTH MINDSET

1. Acknowledge and embrace weaknesses.
2. Don't seek approval; focus on what you want.
3. Use failures and challenges as opportunities to grow.
4. Have an attitude of determination and perseverance.
5. Believe that success is talent plus hard work.

MANAGE THE FEAR

Fear is life's number one killer of growth and success. Fear is the reason that the 98% choose comfort and is something that most people let stop them from moving forward. Fear of the unknown most often holds people captive to their jobs or to their current stage in life. We all have fear. Some people learn to manage their fear better than others. Remember, fear isn't real—it's FEAR (False Evidence Appearing Real). Fear is based in stories made up in your head, in your subconscious. I want to challenge you to never choose comfort, never choose to stay the same, never choose to stay and be comfortable where you are. Never give up on being your best you. Why? All the magic happens outside your comfort zone.

To grow, you have to be in places and situations you haven't been. Pushing yourself to the edge and stretching your limits—conquering your fears—will move you forward. Your comfort zone holds you back. Use your vision to pull you forward and suspend your disbelief. If you can do that, you can simply focus on moving forward.

What are people afraid of primarily? They are afraid of three things: failure, rejection, and success. It is important to understand, however, that everything you want is on the other side of fear. What are you most afraid of? In the pages ahead, I challenge you to embrace your fears and change your mindset about what is possible. Don't overthink success. Instead of focusing on the fear, focus on taking action by using proven models for success.

1. FEAR OF FAILURE

How do you overcome your fear? The first thing you have to do is choose to use your fear as fuel to take action. When I had my successful lawn business, I pulled into the same gas station where I filled up my equipment every day, and a truck came up and parked next to me. I recognized the person in the truck. His name was Terry. He rolled down his window. "Hey, Hoss," he said. "You're still mowing, huh?" I nodded affirmatively to his question. He chuckled and asked, "When are you going to get a real job?"

At that moment, I made the subconscious decision that I would never get a "real" job. And what made him be able to decide for me what a real job was anyway? I wanted to be unemployable. I did not ever want to go to work for somebody else. To me, going to work for somebody else would mean that I had failed. Right there, a fear of failure was born, and to this day it has been a huge driver for me.

Years later, I attended a friend's wedding, and Terry was singing a completely different tune. He had come upon some hard times and actually asked me for a job. I tell you that story because you need to have an internal enemy that drives you—something that's fear to its core. Who is it that you're fighting against, that you're proving wrong? Have you had a competitor who has said you're never going to be able to break into this market? Have they told you something would not work? Has anyone ever told you to go and get a real job? Who is the internal enemy that you have that you're fighting against that will push and drive you to succeed? You can choose to create your own destiny and take control of your success and live life on your terms, not everyone else's terms. Grab onto the fear and let it drive you. The great Frank Sinatra once said, "The best revenge is massive success."

Stop worrying about what everybody else thinks, says, and does. Focus on running your race. Stay in your lane. If you're better today than you were yesterday, that's success. Embrace it. Focus on the right things, because your mindset is your biggest asset. The way that you think and how you coach yourself are important. Always know that your fear is against you and will get you to doubt yourself into not taking action. Fear is Satan himself saying, "No, you cannot go out there and develop your potential and become the best you that you can be. You can't do it. You don't have the right family, and you don't live in the right area. You don't have enough money, you don't have enough education, and you're not smart enough." I used to think that I wasn't smart enough, but now I know that was just an excuse I told myself to not be successful. It was rooted by a fear of failure.

I'm reminded of an encounter I had a few years ago in an elevator. It was back when I had my real estate office. I was running and gunning, and I did a lot of training. I always had people coming up to me asking me questions and picking my brain. One day I was busy running to a listing appointment when a young kid blocked the elevator door, then got on with me. He shook my hand, told me his name, and said, "Hey, Hoss, I'm seventeen years old, I'm getting my license, and I'm going to be the youngest real estate agent in the state of Texas. What is your advice to me?"

I remember thinking how young that was as I contemplated my advice. This is what I told him: "You really need to learn the business from someone experienced. You need to learn the ropes. Find a good team and learn from the team." I was taking into consideration that this kid was young and inexperienced. He took that advice as a "how dare you moment," and determined to be super successful on his own. He went on to be one of the top individual agents in Texas over the next two years. It taught me not to underestimate anybody from that moment forward. It taught me that anybody can do this business if they set out to do it and are willing to work for it. It doesn't matter if you're 17 or 80.

If you have failed at something in the past, dropped the ball, or missed the mark on your goals, this is your moment. Write down what you learned from that experience. How do you get back up and move forward?

2. FEAR OF REJECTION

The next fear is fear of rejection. Fear of rejection is something that many agents let stop them. I want to share with you something that will absolutely destroy the fear of rejection. Think of your role as simply offering your services to the marketplace. That's all you're doing. When you're doing that, to get over the fear of rejection, start asking more questions. Get them on the phone and ask more questions. Dig deep. There's nothing to reject. You are controlling the conversation when you are asking questions based on their answers. Take the conversation three levels deep, find three pains, and provide three solutions to those pains. Don't let them have control. Whoever is in control wins. That's the reason the more direct you are, the more conversions you will get, because you come from a higher level of authority, which is perceived as control.

Change the way you do things that cause rejection, and you will begin to win. Go out there and get better at this. Become more confident. Don't let the fear stop you -- you don't have the fear of rejection! That person doesn't define you. That person who hangs up doesn't define if you're good or you're not. They don't even know you. Don't let them matter. If somebody doesn't like you, who cares?

Stand by your values, defend them, and let that be the thing that holds you up. You have to keep that in your head and play that game every day because if you don't, your fear is going to start creeping in whenever they start "rejecting" you. That's how you overcome your fear of rejection—by defining who you are. It's all about confidence, and managing your fears is going to make you more confident. Fake it until you make it if you have to, but don't let the fear of rejection stop you from taking action.

3. FEAR OF SUCCESS

What about fear of success? Have you ever known anybody who seemed to have it all, and it seemed like they were unknowingly sabotaging themselves? Why do you think people are afraid of success? There are multiple reasons, but I'd like to examine some of the most common. One reason people fear success is because they don't believe they can handle it. Either they have put self-limiting beliefs on themselves or someone else in their life has planted the seeds that if they did become successful, they wouldn't know how to deal with it or sustain it—that it would be over their head, which would then lead to ultimate failure again.

Another reason people are afraid of success is that they are afraid it will change them. Change is oftentimes a good thing, but we have all seen those athletes or actors who couldn't handle all the pressure that came with success. People are often afraid to succeed for the same reason. They're afraid of what they will mess up along the way. Other times people are afraid to succeed because they are afraid it will take too much of them and that they will have to give up too much in return. They might think about losing out on family time or compromising the quality of their relationships. They may be afraid of success becoming too consuming. Remember that being a real estate agent means you are self-employed, so you ultimately call the shots. You get to set the boundaries.

I had a client one time who was very un-coachable. No matter what, he just wouldn't pick up the phone to generate leads. He could barely get out of bed every day. He wanted it, he knew his vision, but we wasn't doing the activity. I asked him what was keeping him from going out and doing what needed to be done—something was stopping him. He said, "I don't know, I just feel like something's stopping me. Maybe … fear?" I broke it down with him because I want you to understand this.

What I've learned through reading, coaching, and working with mentors and coaches personally is that we are often a product of our many experiences growing up where something happened that made such an impact then that today we are experiencing feelings from those events. I asked him who he looked up to for acceptance as a kid, and he told me his grandfather. I asked how much his grandfather made every year, and he said he thought about $50,000. I then asked about where his father was, and he said, "He was busy working. He dropped us off all the time and was too busy for us." When I asked him how that made him feel, he said that he hated it, that he was resentful, and that he couldn't stand that his dad was never there because he was always working.

"So was he self-employed?" I asked.

"No, he worked for somebody else."

"Do you think maybe you anchor working hard with not making much money and not being there for your loved ones?"

My client got quiet for a moment, then acknowledged that was exactly what he did. "If I work hard," he said, "it wouldn't matter anyway because I wouldn't make more money, and I would just be letting my family down in the process."

Right there, everything changed for him because once we knew what was stopping him, we could fix the problem. And we fixed it. The difference between being self-employed and working for somebody else is you are rewarded based on the effort you bring. You're rewarded based on the value. So if you're paying the price every day, and you're out there lead generating every single day, you will be rewarded. I've never met a real estate agent who was broke who lead generated for three hours a day.

MY PERSONAL PHILOSOPHY

Oftentimes, fear just keeps you comfortable. Think about it. We are often looking for things or situations to reinforce our stance of a fixed mindset. It's born from an uncertainty of the future. The choices you make today will either fuel your fear of the future or extinguish it. If you're not prospecting today and not doing the things today that will give you appointments tomorrow, you probably have some anxiety about where your next closing is going to come from. It's a fear. If you're eating or drinking the wrong things today, it will create anxiety and uncertainty of the future. But if you're working out, exercising, and eating the right things, there's nothing to be afraid of. The future will be born from your actions in the now. Focus on today, and that will determine your level of success or failure.

My personal philosophy on business may surprise you, but business to me is nothing but a vehicle chosen to fund your life. My business is not my life. I do my business because that's my passion and what I love to do, but it doesn't control me or own me. It is not something that I'm going to let take precedence over my family or my spirituality. You don't owe real estate your life. It's important to look at it like that because it will help you build your business and your dreams; along with that will come freedom if you do it right.

YOU 2.0

In looking at today, some of you are at the top of your game, and some of you are on your way to the top of your game. Everybody's at a different level of success in his or her business. One thing is for sure: for you to get from where you are right now to the next place you want to be, you've got to do things differently than you've done before. And to do that, you've got to change your thinking. I know that at every single level I've ever been, this has been the case. The more you can understand that, the more you can embrace change. Change is so important. To be able to change on a dime and be able to welcome and get comfortable with it takes knowing more about your current mindset and personal philosophies.

Why is it so critical to understand and *change* your personal philosophies? Your personal philosophy controls your thoughts, your thoughts control your actions, your actions determine your results, and your results determine your beliefs. Let's start by exploring your personal power and what that means to you. Having been a self-employed entrepreneur all my life and having helped agents around the country explode to the next level, I've realized that there is a common theme among us—each of us believes we have a better version of us inside ourselves, no matter where we are today. That's our personal power. If you want to have the mindset of a top producer, you must understand that what you want is to manage getting on the other side of your fear so you can reach the next level. My goal is to help you unleash that person. You 2.0 is not going to show up on your doorstep one morning looking for you; you have to go out there and create that person.

Let me ask you this question: "Do you compete to win or do you compete to *not lose*?" This question will help you understand the "why." Why are you competing, why are you setting goals, and why do you want to achieve whatever it is you want to achieve? You never really lose; you only win or learn.

If you're the person who says, "I compete to not lose," I can already tell how you're going to be in a negotiation. Will the outcome be a win-win? Probably not, because the result comes from a scarcity framework instead of one of abundance, meaning that you think there is a limited supply of winning. You want to embrace abundance by changing your mindset. There is more business out there than you can possibly ever get. Seriously, you can get all that you desire. There's no shortage of money to earn, no shortage of homes to sell, no shortage of books to read, no shortage of mentors and coaches, and they can all help you find answers to give you what you want. But it comes down to you. You've got to reach deep inside yourself and have a mindset focused on winning.

One thing that I've realized in my quest to become Hoss 2.0, or the best version of me at every level, is there are just some things that are hard to answer or understand. That's okay. When I moved to Dallas in my early twenties, I didn't know anyone, and I didn't fully understand the people who would come into my life or the opportunities I would be given. I cannot explain how I would meet someone at just the right time or read a book that had the exact message I needed to hear at that moment. What I do understand and have learned is that in taking action and going for it (your dreams and where you want to be), you've got to have a lot of faith.

There is a personal power in making the statement that "I am." In 2008, there was the biggest disruption to the US housing market since the Great Depression. Primary causes for the crash included low mortgage interest rates, adjustable-rate mortgages, relaxed standards for mortgage loans, and lower down payments. I looked into the mirror and said, "I am not participating in this recession," and I believed it. The next two years were the best two years of my life financially. Everything that comes after "I am" is true of yourself. What is your inner self-talk? What do you say to yourself? Are you your biggest fan or your biggest critic? Are you somebody that's always talking to yourself and getting yourself fired up? One thing that I love to do is wake up in the morning and remind myself what "I am." This is what I say:

I am blessed. I am well able. I am successful.
I am victorious. I am talented. I am creative.
I am wise. I am healthy. I am in shape. I am energetic.
I am happy. I am positive.
I am passionate. I am strong. I am confident. I am secure.
I am beautiful. I am attractive.
I am valuable. I am free. I am redeemed. I am forgiven.
I am anointed. I am accepted.
I am approved. I am prepared. I am qualified.
I am motivated. I am focused.
I am disciplined. I am determined. I am patient.
I am kind. I am generous. I am excellent.
I am equipped. I am empowered. I am prosperous. I am loved.

What is your "I am" self-talk? You need to become your biggest fan to realize that you can become anything your heart desires. I challenge you to make a list of your "I am" statements and repeat them to yourself every day. Add your top five "I am" statements to your weekly goals. Own them. Stake your claim to them. Remind yourself of your worthiness.

One thing one-percenters have in common is repeating affirmations to themselves. I learned that from my mentors and coaches. Every single one of them taught me the power of affirmations. When I made my first list, I remember thinking it was silly (I thought the same thing about journaling). I've learned, though, that it was just because it was new, and I didn't understand the value until my affirmations became habits. There's magic to putting the ink to the paper. There's power behind it that is difficult to explain. It's like tithing. You can't explain how it works, but if you have tithed anyway out of obedience to your faith, then you've experienced the blessings and know it's the best thing you can possibly do for your financial destiny.

PERSONAL GROWTH

One of the most important keys for changing your mindset is to have a mindset focused on continual personal growth. To be successful, you don't want things that just last 60 days or a year or even a decade. You want to be doing things that will last a lifetime, and it begins with knowing how to succeed.

I love the parable of the Chinese bamboo tree. Like any plant, the bamboo tree requires watering, good soil, and sunshine. There is no sign of activity the first year. Again, in the second year, there is no growth above the soil line. The third and fourth years still yield nothing. You are impatient and beginning to wonder if you're ever going to see the fruit of your labor. Finally, in the fifth year, a miracle happens. Growth happens, and not just any growth. The tree grows 80 feet in just a few weeks. How is that possible? Because the strength of its roots sustained its life and helped to overcome obstacles and challenges. Because the foundation was virtually unshakable. That's what personal growth is like; that's what long-lasting success looks like. You want to establish your roots so when you experience adversity and obstacles, you are left standing.

FOUR LEVELS OF LEARNING

According to the Johari Window, there are four levels of learning, and every one of us, in everything that we encounter and endeavor, are in various stages of these four levels in every area of our lives. Many of you have heard of it before, but it is worthy of repeating.

LEVEL 1. DON'T KNOW (UNCONSCIOUS INCOMPETENCE)

You don't know what you don't know, so keep an open mind. If you aren't careful, you can get stuck here in a state of complacency where you never question your current thinking. Don't build a know-it-all wall and shut yourself off from receiving. The finding is reserved for the seekers.

LEVEL 2. KNOW (CONSCIOUS INCOMPETENCE)

You know what you don't know, and it may even make you uncomfortable. Knowing is awareness. Knowing, however, and not doing, doesn't serve you. You have to put into practice what you know. That's where the rubber hits the road. Once you put your knowledge into practice, it becomes a skill and an asset.

LEVEL 3. EXPERIENCE (CONSCIOUS COMPETENCE)

This is the most important part of the four levels of learning. Conscious competence is knowing that you know how to do something. This is the experience. For example, you can read prospecting scripts all day long, practice them, and know them inside and out. But until you put the scripts into practice and experience them in the real world, knowing them gains you nothing. You must reach the point at which you experience those scripts in the marketplace at such a level that it becomes conscious incompetence—where you don't even have to think about it, the scripts roll off your tongue, and you can tie your shoes without thinking about it. You've got to work on the experience before it becomes a skill. You have to put in the work.

> YOU MUST BECOME A SKILLIONAIRE BEFORE YOU CAN BECOME A MILLIONAIRE.

LEVEL 4. SKILL (UNCONSCIOUS COMPETENCE)

You know how to do something, and it is second nature. You rock at it. The skill is where the reward is on the other side of that experience. Here's why this is so important: It's the success gap between where you are right now and where you want to be. The success gap exists at every level. There's a lot you don't know, resources you don't have, money you don't have, people you don't know, skills you don't have in the success gap. Respect the gap. The answer in closing the gap is in personal development.

What skills—if you focused on them in the next 12 months and could develop them—would allow you to have exponential increases in your business? It's always important to know what those skills are. Knowing gives you power.

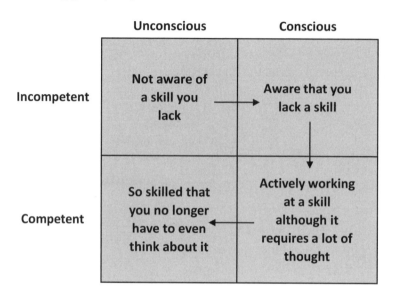

INVEST IN YOURSELF

Every year I'm at a different level because of the people in my life, things I'm aware of, and things I've learned. A big reason this has happened in my life is because I've always invested in myself. If you look at my library, I have accumulated more books than most people have in a lifetime. I'm 35 years old as of this writing, and I have over 1,300 books. I invest in everything. When I go to a seminar, I'm the biggest buyer in the room. I invest in coaching. I do this because I don't know what I need to know today to get to where I'm going to be, and the bridge between those two are those books, those products, or the knowledge I don't yet have. I'm going to take that knowledge that I

> INVEST IN AS MUCH OF YOURSELF AS YOU CAN; YOU ARE BY FAR YOUR OWN BIGGEST ASSET.
>
> –WARREN BUFFET

don't have and I'm going to apply it to action (or experience) where it becomes a skill. Warren Buffet says, "Invest in as much of yourself as you can; you are by far your own biggest asset."

Virtually every highly successful person invests in himself or herself. They don't consider hiring a coach as an expense versus an investment. I pay a fortune for coaching, but that's the only way my income goes up every year.

CHANGE YOUR STORY, CHANGE YOUR RESULTS

Your story is everything you've experienced up until this point, and it is built on your beliefs. The only reason you aren't where you want to be is the BS story you tell yourself about why you aren't there. Did you ever stop to think about why you believe the things you believe or think the way you do? It is all about your roots. Beliefs grow deep from your history, your childhood, your role models, and everything that you were ever told. Your experiences, your teaching, your religion, your colleagues, your friends, and your family establish your beliefs. The trouble is that over time, things change. Times change. Not everything, but some things. If you never examine why you believe what you do or think the way you do, you won't make the change you need to in order to do differently.

Just as we discussed, you need to do different things every time you are moving to get to a next level. At every level you've got to change your beliefs again. You've got to change what you think you know. This is so important because your story is built from your beliefs, and you're 100% responsible for them. Your only limitations are the ones you put on yourself. What determines your beliefs?

ENVIRONMENT

You become a product of your environment. Make sure your environment is a positive influence for you. If I had not reached out to my mentor Jimbo, who spoke some sense into me when I was discouraged, I wouldn't be here today. It's important to have people like

Jimbo in your environment to tell you what you need to know when you need to know it to help you get out of your own way when you want to quit. It's important to have truth tellers. Truth tellers are the people who will tell you what you don't want to hear in your life because you become a product of your environment. I challenge you to look around and see who's in your life, in your business, and who you are spending your time with. Are these people talking positive or negative, are they encouraging or discouraging, do they empower you or tear you down? You need people in your life who believe in you even when you don't believe in yourself. Surround yourself with doers—those people who make it happen and don't make excuses.

Be willing to downsize your environment to eliminate negative forces. I have high standards, and the environment and group of people I choose to spend my time around is pretty small.

EVENTS

Events and the things that have happened to you in the past form your beliefs. When I didn't sell anything my first six months when I got into real estate, it was brutal. I got hung up on more than once. People did not call me back. I got rejected at every level. It began to build my belief of why I was not made to be a real estate agent. But that was a lie. Events and things that happen in your life don't matter. What matters is how you react and realign to those events. Those events should empower you, not stop you. The events in your life should only have the meaning you give them.

KNOWLEDGE

The other thing that forms your beliefs is knowledge—what you know or what you don't know. As I said from the beginning, you are the same person today that you're going to be in five years except for the people you meet and the books that you read. How much are you going to grow in the next five years? Your goal is to gain knowledge because gaining knowledge creates awareness. Remember that knowledge is an ever-moving thing. Just because you know something to be true today does not mean it will be true five years from now. Things change. Market conditions change. Many factors will change over time, so keep up with innovations and how things change.

RESULTS

The last thing that helps to form your beliefs is results. Anything you've actually done and accomplished shapes your beliefs. If you take 30 listings in 30 days, then you believe you can do that. If you convert a prospect on the phone, you know you can do that.

You've got to self-assess what you need to change. What's holding you back? Changing your beliefs will help you change your story, and when you change your story, you truly change your results. What's the story you're telling yourself on a daily basis? What's the story you believe, the story you're fighting for, the story you're running from? What's the story that encourages you and that drives you every single day? Your success story—you 2.0—is on the other side of action. If you want to be the best you possible, you have to make changes and take action.

Remember that success occurs when your dreams get bigger than your excuses. Mindset is everything.

 ACTIONS TO TAKE

1. Create your "I am" list.
2. Examine your beliefs and write down areas where you need to change your story.
3. Create a plan to continue your personal growth.

 KEYS TO SUCCESS

1. Desire is the birthplace of motivation.
2. There are two kinds of mindsets. There is a fixed mindset and a growth mindset. To be successful, you want to have a growth mindset.
3. Remember, fear isn't real. FEAR is False Evidence Appearing Real. Fear is stories made up in your head, in your subconscious.

4. Oftentimes, fear just keeps you comfortable, born out of a fear of the unknown future.

5. Your personal philosophy controls your thoughts, and your thoughts and actions control your destiny.

6. Fortune favors those bold enough to move beyond their fear and step out before they have all the answers. Follow your life's purpose without questioning why. Keep moving forward, and here's what will happen ... the right people will come into your life at the right time. Be fearless in this pursuit.

7. Changing your beliefs will help you change your story, and when you change your story, you truly change your results.

8. Success occurs when your dreams get bigger than your excuses.

3. Maximize Your Time and Effort

People often complain about lack of time
when it is their lack of direction that is the problem.
—Zig Ziglar

One area in life where every person has a level playing field is time. Everyone has the same amount, every day. Today life moves fast, and there are many distractions. Learning to leverage and maximize your time and efforts will allow you to make room for all the things you want from life, and it will help you become more successful.

You have to start taking action on managing your time better, because action creates habit. Repetition breeds mastery. Time is an asset, and it is important to treat it that way.

TIME IS AN ASSET, AND IT IS IMPORTANT TO TREAT IT THAT WAY.

HIGH-LEVERAGE ACTIVITIES (HLAs)

How many people do you know, including yourself, who let themselves be controlled by their schedule? How often do you hear people complaining about just not having enough time to do the things they need to do? What I want to show you is how to take the same 24 hours you have each day and leverage it to your advantage instead of being controlled by it. Leveraging your time becomes your differentiator and your catalyst for achieving exponential results. My hope is that by the end of this chapter, you will have a completely different mindset about how time is your biggest asset and that leveraging it is one of the top keys to your success.

I like to think of time in terms of getting paid. Stop and think about all the things you did yesterday. Write them down. Write down everything from the time you got out of bed until you got back into bed, and put an approximate time allotment next to each one. How many minutes did you spend on activities that were money-making activities? What does that translate to in terms of percentage of your time? Did you spend even 50% of your time generating revenue? If you amortized your percentage over a day, a month, and a year, how would that serve you towards reaching your vision and goals? Chances are, you would fall way short unless you have some strong systems and disciplines in place to ensure you are staying focused on things that make you money. How long do you think it will take to become a $20-million agent doing $20-an-hour tasks?

What if you spent 70% or more of your work time in money-making activities, or what I call High-Leverage Activities? How different do you think your results would be? What is a High-Leverage Activity? They are the activities that maximize the efficiency and effectiveness of your time, money, and relationships.Identifying those activities and scheduling your time accordingly will dramatically affect your results.

As a real estate agent, I want you to think about time as it relates to your business. The activities that provide the highest leverage lead generation, following proven systems to convert leads, and investing in your personal growth so you become more valuable. My experience tells me, however, that 95% of real estate agents will spend the majority of their time focused on paperwork. It's amazing how many agents don't even lead generate at all. Many don't prospect. Too often people get mired down in those things that are urgent but not important tasks that they end up filling their whole days with before they even realize it.

How much of your time is spent being strategic versus tactical? When things get busy, most people tend to work way too heavily in tactical and not enough in strategic. What you need is a balance between the two, but most people don't take the time to be strategic. With a plan that is focused only on strategy that will help you realize your vision, you will almost always fall short. Figure out what your top HLA's are and block your time so you spend the majority of your time working in that zone. Below are some of the top HLA's in real estate. These are the top four activities that support revenue generation and long-term growth:

- Prospecting

- Presenting

- Building Relationships

- Leading

That's it. Those are the activities you need to focus on. You might say, "I'm inputting a listing." No, stop doing that. "I'm in a team meeting, and I'm motivating my buyer agents and my assistant." Great, that's leading. "I'm doing a virtual listing presentation." Great, that's presenting. Stop justifying doing other things that don't make you money.

Remember to ask yourself every day, "Is what I'm doing right now a money-making activity?"

RESPECT YOUR TIME

I've studied successful people over time, and I was meeting recently with a very busy, successful speaker/author. We were talking about managing time, and he showed me his schedule. He time-blocked everything. In addition to those important money-making activities, he even scheduled when he meditated, when he ate breakfast, when he spent time reading, and when he worked out. He scheduled family time so it would not get left out, especially on extra busy weeks. What this extreme discipline allowed him was to reduce distractions and just get more done. Period. What I found particularly interesting in his schedule was he included all the important elements to support him in his pursuit of being his best version of himself. He included HLA's, things to sharpen his mind, self-improvement activities to make himself more valuable, things to keep him strong health-wise, and solid time with the people he loves in his life.

IS WHAT I'M DOING RIGHT NOW A MONEY-MAKING ACTIVITY?

In addition to helping him better own his time by scheduling it out, often to the minute, it also allowed him to do something else that was beautiful. He learned to say no to more things that did not support using his time productively. Being self-employed takes a huge amount of discipline, especially when people around you take that to mean you are more easily interrupted than someone who works in the corporate world. They oftentimes don't place the same value on your time, so it is important that you place the importance on your time. If you don't, you will let other people spend it foolishly.

Does that mean you should never allow yourself to work outside of your schedule or that you should say no to everything outside your priorities? Probably not, but it does mean that nobody else will care about the best use of your time more than you. Don't give it up just because someone asks you to. If a friend calls to talk in the middle of the day, ask if you can call them back in the evening. You don't have to put them off altogether, but you need to be a good steward of your time. If you don't, it will be gone, and you can never get those minutes back. Own them. Use them wisely. People will respect you for it, especially when they see how your discipline turns into success. Live your life by design, not by accident.

LIVE YOUR LIFE BY DESIGN, NOT BY ACCIDENT.

OWN YOUR TIME

A somewhat different perspective on respecting your time is owning your time. If you have already learned to say no and you block your time for the things that are the most important to you, then how else can you leverage your time to maximize your efforts? The answer is to own your time.

I want to challenge you here to realize ways that you can literally "find" an extra 10-20 hours per week if you are willing to change your mindset. What are ways you can gain extra time?

One of the simplest ways to gain extra time is to get up early. Setting your alarm a half hour earlier will gain you three and a half hours a week or an extra 182 hours in a year. That's like gaining over 7.5 days a year with that one move. As I previously stated, you can't be a $20-million agent if your time is spent focused on $20-an-hour activities. Determine those things that need to be done, but don't have to be done by you, and prioritize the things that you can delegate to other people. This can be clerical tasks, errands you need someone to run for you, mowing the yard, cleaning your house, and other things that do not specifically require your direct participation that are currently keeping you from maximizing your time. Let me give you a visual on this.

WHAT IS YOUR TIME WORTH?

Annual Salary	Hourly Rate Equivalent
$50K	$25
$100K	$50
$200K	$100
$500K	$250

What is your time worth? Take your salary, and look at the hourly rate equivalent. If I make $250 an hour, is it a good use of my time to mow my lawn? No, I should hire someone to do that. If it takes me two hours to mow my lawn, and I can pay someone $100, how much money have I lost if I do it myself? I lose the equivalent of $400 ($500 earned = $100 spent). Think about how you're spending your time, and make a commitment to hire and/or delegate those things that are keeping you from reaching your full potential.

Another major tip for owning your time is to simply stop doing things that have no value, things that take time but add no value or revenue back. It doesn't matter if it's something that's always been done. Don't be afraid to just let it go completely.

Be determined to be the owner of your time and say how and when it is spent. I believe that by implementing these concepts and creating your Daily Method of Operations, you could potentially gain an extra 30-40% more time just by maximizing the same amount of hours spent and getting creative on how to get things executed. If you take that 30% and apply it 100% to High-Leverage Activities, what could that do to your revenue over the next year? Let's build that blueprint.

You all know by now that I'm a big fan of Jim Rohn. In fact, I like to say that my dad and family raised me as a kid, and Jim Rohn raised me as an adult. His philosophies turned things around for me. Here's one of his truths that has had the biggest impact on me:

If you want to have more, you have to become more.
For things to change, you have to change.
For things to get better, you have to get better.
For things to improve, you have to improve.
If you grow, everything grows for you.

DAILY METHOD OF OPERATIONS

Now, I want to pull this all together for you and help you create your daily method of operations. The reason I want you to do this exercise is so you can create habits for yourself that include accomplishing all the things that are important to you and so you can truly maximize your time and effort. To give you perspective, I want to share with you my personal daily method of operations, and then I want you to create your own. As I share with you my day, I want to expand on why each one is important to me so you can use the same mindset as you create your own.

DAILY METHOD OF OPERATIONS

5:25	Wake up. Enjoy an attitude of gratitude. Get out of bed.
5:35	Drink water. Take vitamins. Stretch. Do push-ups and sit-ups.
6:00	Shower and dress.
6:30	Eat breakfast, read goals, and plan day.
7:00	Share quality time with family.
7:30	Read (20 minutes).
7:50	Journal (10 minutes).
8:00	Focus on work and lead prep.
9:00	Prospect. Utilize alter ego, dial for dollars, smile and dial.
Noon	Eat lunch, stretch, and get outside. Renew energy.
1:00	Conduct required business. Check emails, return calls, negotiate deals.
4:00	Complete listing appointments/prospect. If no appointments, then prospect.
8:00	Relax. Spend time with family. Read.

10:00   Read goals, review day, read. Sleep.

Let me remind you that this is MY daily method of operations and that you can take from it the things that make sense and then build your own perfect day that works for you. Make it your own. Everything here is important to me. I follow this Monday through Friday. I encourage you to replace things that aren't the same for you with things that are important in your life. As you create this day, think in terms of "if I repeat this day every day as closely as possible, I will have tremendous success."

> THE FEW WHO
> DO ARE THE
> ENVY OF THE
> MANY WHO
> ONLY WATCH.
> –JIM ROHN

5:25 A.M. (10 MINUTES)

My day starts at 5:25 a.m. This is a choice I make. Why? Because statistics show that highly successful people rise by 6:00 a.m. And I know that if I want to be successful, I have to model successful people. This is something I can control, and it doesn't take any learning or skill to make it happen. It just takes a choice.

The first thing I do every day is spend 10 minutes in bed having an attitude of gratitude. What's this? I'm thankful for the things in life I've been given and for the opportunities I have before me. I live a blessed life, and I remind myself every day to be grateful. Then I'm out of bed and ready for the day.

5:35 A.M. (25 MINUTES)

At 5:35 a.m., I drink water and take vitamins. Vitamins are important for your health, and the healthier you are, the more energy you have to perform. Next, I stretch and spend a half hour doing push-ups and sit-ups. For me, exercise gets my adrenaline pumping in the morning.

6:00 A.M. (30 MINUTES)

At 6:00 a.m., I'm out of bed, groomed, and dressed for the day.

When you think about the clothes you choose to wear for the day, think about what makes you feel good about yourself. Some people function better when they are more dressed up, others are more productive when they wear appropriate comfortable clothes. Make intentional choices that help you maximize your time and effort.

6:30 A.M. (30 MINUTES)

At 6:30 in the morning, I review my goals and planning for the day while I have some breakfast. I look at the previous day and transfer over anything that did not get accomplished. Make other adjustments as needed, but be intentional about what you want to accomplish that day.

7:00 A.M. (30 MINUTES)

For me, 7:00 a.m. is family time. This is when I get to visit with my wife and spend quality time with my daughters. During this time, all my focus is on the favorite women in my life, my wife and three daughters. I show an interest in them and what they care about because it is important to me and they are important to me.

7:30 A.M. (20 MINUTES)

At 7:30, I read for about 20 minutes for personal growth. Grab a good book, and just read. Underline things that resonate with you, take notes, write down your Aha moments. Commit to reading every day, and finish what you start. I wasn't born enjoying to read by a long shot. I barely made it through high school. But at 22, I decided that reading was a way to learn from others and make myself more valuable to the world.

7:50 A.M. (10 MINUTES)

For me, the 10 minutes I spend journaling from 7:50 to 8:00 in the morning are some of the most powerful minutes spent in my day. I encourage you to journal daily. Journaling is very important because you have to get your thoughts out of your head. You will feel a lot more at peace when you journal. I wish I had begun journaling when my mentors and coaches first tried to impress on me the value, but I now understand, and I make journaling a part of my daily habits and activity.

8:00 A.M. (60 MINUTES)

From 8:00 a.m. to 9:00 a.m., I focus. I focus on my day and any other prep I need to do to set myself up for success. Use this time to pull leads from your lead provider, review them, practice your calls and scripts, and be ready when it is time to lead generate.

9:00 A.M. (180 MINUTES)

At 9:00 a.m., start lead generation. Be prospecting, making phone calls, smiling and dialing. Get yourself in the right state and just go for it. For three hours, be disciplined in making sure you are actively seeking business. This is the single biggest thing you can do to leverage your time because it makes money.

People ask me why I lead generate in the morning specifically. For me, it's when my energy is highest, and I believe that I will be less likely to put it off if I put it at the beginning of my day. When I make my calls, people can hear the energy in my voice. When I prospect in the afternoons, I often don't have the same energy level. I prefer to be a maker in the morning and a manager in the afternoon.

Do what works for you. I highly recommend you do your prospecting at your highest energy times of the day. This is the most important activity you have, so set yourself up to succeed.

NOON (60 MINUTES)

I typically don't take a lunch hour. If I do, it might be on the fly. I might grab a protein shake or a light lunch and spend the bulk of the hour either continuing my prospecting or use that time to get caught up on other activities. I may respond to emails, return some calls, or review the morning calls and see if there are things I need to follow up on.

And by the way, as an agent, I didn't work Saturdays and Sundays, and I still don't work Saturdays and Sundays. I hang out with my family and spend time with them, because that's what I like to do on the weekends. But the reason I like to do that is because I'm so effective during the week. Following this schedule will be highly effective and make you highly productive.

1:00 P.M. (180 MINUTES)

After lunch take care of business activities. Check email, return phone calls, and negotiate deals as needed. Communicate with lenders during this time. This is where the paperwork will come in that will need to be handle. Running an efficient business is important, and there are many activities that truly need to be done. Just make sure it takes its appropriate time and space in your day.

4:00 P.M. (120-180 MINUTES)

From 4:00 p.m. until 6:00 or 7:00 p.m., go on listing appointments. What if someone wants a listing appointment at 1:00 p.m.? I don't care. Stay focused on lead generation when it is blocked on your schedule. Learn to tell people no. It will set you up as an authority to not always be available.

In Dr. Robert Cialdini's book, *Influence* there is a principle called the Authority Principle. People respect authority. They want to follow the lead of real experts. If you let your clients completely control your schedule, they will not respect you or your time, and chances are if you are always available, they will not truly appreciate you as an expert. Tell people no and offer up alternative times that fit within your schedule. Quit trying to be a puppet on a string and please everybody; you can't please everybody. Don't be afraid to tell people no.

If you don't have appointments for this time, get back on the phone. Get back to lead generating. Return to doing the money-making activities.

7:00 P.M. UNTIL BEDTIME

My evenings are spent working out, having dinner, and enjoying family time with my wife and daughters, and then I find time for some additional reading. In addition, I review the day and see where I stand on accomplishing the goals I set out that morning. What did I do? How did I feel? What did I learn? What can I do tomorrow that no one will expect from me?

One of my favorite quotes from Jim Rohn is "The few who do are the envy of the many who only watch." Be a doer. Have you ever heard that it's lonely at the top? I have, and, it *is* lonely at the top. I'll tell you why. Most people don't want you up there. They want you down with them. It makes them uncomfortable for you to be an overachiever. Pushing yourself and holding yourself to a higher standard can be intimidating to others. Don't worry about what everybody else says. Just be the best you that you can be every day.

So how do you create and follow your own perfect day to get the results that you want? The answer is, you just decide. The reason people make decisions, right or wrong, is their willingness to avoid pain and gain pleasure. Repetition breeds mastery. In anything you do, if you don't do it consistently, you won't get consistent results.

Build your perfect day. Using the model I laid out for you with my own, create your own perfect day. It will become your new standard for yourself. It will be your blueprint for building the structure that will lead to achieving your goals. Take it one day at a time, and if you have a bad day, start over again tomorrow. There are no limits to starting over. Be committed to the process and your system. Use technology to keep things automatic and systematized. Set timers and reminders.

☞ ACTIONS TO TAKE

1. Identify your High-Leverage Activities.
2. Build your Daily Method of Operations that supports personal growth, spending time with people who are important to you, and focus on those High-Leverage Activities that help you achieve your goals.
3. Determine those things you are currently doing that you can delegate to others (even if you have to pay them) so you can benefit exponentially by gaining those hours.

KEYS TO SUCCESS

1. You have to start taking action on managing your time better because action creates habit. Repetition breeds mastery. Time is an asset, and it is important to treat it that way.

2. Live your life by design, not by accident.

3. You can literally "find" an extra 10-20 hours per week if you are willing to change your mindset and follow a daily method of operations.

4. Do your prospecting at your highest energy times of the day. This is the most important activity you have, so set yourself up to succeed.

5. It bears repeating ... repetition breeds mastery.

6. Join **Listing Boss Academy**. See my invitation on page 201

4. Identify Your Niches

Everyone is not your customer.
Recognize that you can't cater to everyone.
You have to find your niche.
—Seth Godin

W e're all one piece of information away from achieving any level of success that we want to achieve. That's why we can't ever stop our pursuit of excellence. While I hope you will have many epiphanies throughout this book that will change the way you think and how you execute moving forward, this one can change everything for you.

YOUR BUSINESS CAN'T BE ALL THINGS TO ALL PEOPLE AND EXCEL AT ANYTHING.

Your business can't be all things to all people and excel at anything. Every entrepreneur and every business needs a strategy to keep them focused. In fact, in this new world of pervasive interactivity, it's time to rethink even how to develop a strategy.

So I want to state up front in this chapter that this one thing can change everything for you. Identify your niches. If you do, you will dramatically change your results.

METS AND HAVEN'T METS

What is the difference in the groups I'm calling the "Mets" and "Haven't Mets"? One group is all the people who you have dealt with professionally or who you know on a personal level. These are your current contacts. You have "met" them. The "Haven't Mets" are specific niches or people you can target, but you have not yet met them. It is important to consider this distinction, because you will market to each group differently. I have identified below examples of those people in each group, but this list is not all-inclusive:

METS	HAVEN'T METS
Sphere of Influence (SOI)	For Sale By Owners (FSBOs)
Past Clients	Expired Leads (Expireds)
Active Listings	Builders
Active Buyers	Farm

The Mets will bring you the most repeat referral business. Depending on the level of the relationships, this can be a tremendous revenue source. Let's examine each group of Mets.

SOI

Your SOI is made up of people that love you, like you, and trust you. When capturing this list, it should be segmented by the level of relationship:

A = Loves you
B = Likes you
C = Knows you

The goal is always to be growing the SOI because this is how your business will grow. These people will call you when they have a real estate need.

PAST CLIENTS

It is critical to have a systematic approach, system, and follow-up campaign, as well as a marketing strategy around your past clients. Recognize the lifetime value of that client. I read a statistic that 78% of sellers said that they would use the same real estate agent again to sell their home, yet less than 10% actually do. I believe this is primarily because agents don't follow up. If you are not top of mind when a need arises, the chances the past client will reach out to you are much smaller than if you have a system for continuing to market to them and stay on their radar. Don't ever let your past clients slip through the cracks and become someone else's clients.

ACTIVE LISTINGS AND ACTIVE BUYER

These are people who have signed a Buyer Representation Agreement (BRA). Typically you have a lot of these. In my active listing campaign, as soon as I put a home on the market, it was like a Disney World experience from that point on, because I had a system for every single seller. I worked hard to get their business, and I wanted to blow them away with how I continue to serve them, so I had a system.

Your Mets are your warm market and are a priority. They have the highest probability of becoming clients because you have a connection of some kind with them already. Everyone should work their Met groups.

Some of you are better with the Haven't Mets. These are your For Sale By Owners, Expireds, Short Sales, and your Neighborhood Farm as examples. These are true niches. These are people who don't know who you are; that's the challenge, and I want to share with you how to get them to respond. How do you position yourself as the expert to this market? And do you spend more time going after the Mets or the Haven't Mets? It depends on your strengths and weaknesses. That is typically determined at least partially by your personality type.

DISC PERSONALITY TYPES

I'm specifically talking with you about the DISC personality styles to help you identify your niches, but knowing them and understanding the personality of the people around you is extremely valuable in knowing how best to communicate and relate to them to get them to respond the way you want them to respond. I encourage you to learn even more than what I'm sharing with you here if you want to be even more effective in all your communication.

Let me use myself as an example. On the DISC scale, I'm a high D with a secondary I. I love marketing to people who don't know me. I like calling people, and I'm a machine at doing it; I'm relentless. If you give me an obstacle, I'm going to plow through it no matter what I have to do to make that happen. My personality is very suited for going after the Haven't Mets, because I'm dominant and direct. I like to negotiate and have the power over the situation. I find my personal advantage and go for it. Ds are more bullet-proof and take rejection better than any other personality type. This is another reason they are typically so successful with the Haven't Mets. If they get rejected, they just move on.

For all of you who fall into the I category, you are influencers. You

DISC Quick Reference Guide

	D		I		S		C	
	DOMINANT/DIRECT		**INFLUENCER**		**STEADY**		**COMPLIANT**	
General Style (When this factor is high)	Assertive	Decisive	Confident	Influential	Patient	Deliberate	Cautious	Logical
	Competitive	Driving	Expressive	Persuasive	Thoughtful	Dependable	Exacting	Systematic
	Direct	Self-starter	Enthusiastic	Friendly	Sympathetic	Predictable	Pragmatic	Conservative
	Risk-taking	Aggressive	Talkative	Charming	Pleasant	Persistent	Organizing	Disciplined
	Ambitious	Forceful	Sociable	Generous	Reliable	Passive	Analytical	Diplomatic
Style Structure (Perception of Situations & Normal Response)	Assertive/Controlled		Assertive/Open		Passive/Open		Passive/Controlled	
	Antagonistic		Favorable		Favorable		Antagonistic	
	Direct and dynamic		Open and expressive		Positive and receptive		Cautious and analytical	
Style Focus	Tangible success		Social interaction		Comfort in surroundings		Detailed understanding	
	Rapid achievement		Self-expression		Personal acceptance		Structure and control	
Motivating Factors	Achievement and success (especially in competition)		Accepting, social environment (especially as center of attention)		Non-demanding environment (especially in a positive team)		Structure and rules (especially under own control)	
Demotivating Factors	Restrictive Bureaucracy		Lack of social acceptance		Urgent, demanding situations		Unpredictable circumstances	
	Frustrated ambitions		Formal conditions		Changes to routine		Need for direct action	
Basic Communication Style	**Informs**		**Discusses**		**Absorbs**		**Analyzes**	
	States requirements and instructions		Enjoys positive communication for its own sake		Tends to listen to others rather than state their own views		Considers statements and tends to concentrate on factual matters	
Leadership Style	**Demands**		**Confers**		**Supports**		**Regulates**	
	Controlling, issues instructions, delegates freely		Discusses decisions with others, looks for approval, fosters team spirit		Provides personal support, open to suggestions and ideas, loyal to the team		Controls through rules, maintains organization, concerned with accurate work	
Sales Style	**Negotiates**		**Enthuses**		**Presents**		**Explains**	
	Presents benefits, not features, builds negotiations, maximizes personal gain		Communicates positively, refers to user experiences, tends to be hesitant in closing		Follows an established pattern, presents steadily and thoroughly, stands by commitments		Presents features, not benefits, focuses on technicalities, provides accurate information	
Sales Strategy	**Power**		**People**		**Promise**		**Proof**	
	Looks for personal advantage		Judges by personal impressions		Trusts personal guarantees		Requires clear understanding	

typically want to please and serve everyone, and you are most comfortable in the Mets group. An I is someone who loves to be in social settings and prefers to pick up the phone and talk to someone they know and who already likes them. An I personality type typically doesn't take rejection well, so it is difficult for them to put themselves in a situation where this is a possibility. That's why is it important to have a plan and a system that will increase your opportunity for success. People with an I personality tend to get the most referrals, because people love them. They are pleasers. I also have a lot of the I personality trait, so I also tend to get a lot of referrals. Some people have just one dominant personality, and others have a very strong secondary.

An S personality leans towards being non-demanding. They are very supportive and will present their ideas in an established way. They are more passive in nature and want to be accepted. The S and C personality styles like to overthink and overanalyze things. They want to be really organized and ready before presenting. The S and C types tend to be much more analytical and give more details. Leverage these traits as strengths and find the niches that respond to your strengths the most. For example, investors need details, information, and organization. That's a great niche for you if these are your strengths.

It is important to understand your own personality style so you can better work to your strengths. If you haven't taken the DISC profile test, I strongly encourage you to. You can take it online, and it is not expensive. Knowing your style and those of your team members also helps you navigate around those weaknesses through awareness. Putting systems into place will help overcome the natural tendencies to shy away from areas just because of your comfort zone. Identify what your strengths are and go after the niche that best suits your dominant trait and personality. Delegate to others those areas that are outside of your strengths in order to balance out your personal niches where possible, but also be willing to challenge yourself to overcome your resistance by putting strong systems into place.

Knowing and understanding personality styles will also help you identify the personalities of your clients and allow you to speak to them in their preferred style. In my case, being a D personality can come on too strong if I don't temper it somewhat. It will turn some personalities off. Use the styles to your benefit both for yourself and to get your clients to respond to you the way you desire.

RICHES IN NICHES

When I started out in real estate and identified my niches, I went from being completely unsuccessful to being highly successful virtually overnight. It gave me focus, and I chose niches that fed to my strengths. It's just that simple.

Just because you can do something doesn't mean you should. There are so many different types of opportunities in the real estate industry. Trying to be great at all of them simultaneously will not allow you to master any of them, and chances are you will be mediocre as a whole. I don't know anyone who wakes up in the morning thinking, "I can't wait to be mediocre today," or, worse yet, "I can't wait to get mediocre results today."

My experience tells me that the riches are in niches. Think about it. Would you rather be a small fish in an ocean or a big fish in a small pond? I prefer to be the Incredible Hulk in a puddle. You can leave a significant impact on a targeted niche.

WOULD YOU RATHER BE A BIG FISH IN A SMALL POND OR A SMALL FISH IN AN OCEAN? THERE ARE RICHES IN NICHES.

You don't need to carve out a niche that no one else has, but it is important to find just a few markets areas where you want to primarily spend your focus. By doing so, you will be able to create strategies, tools, and processes that are very specific to each and maximize your efforts in duplication.

What are the niches in the real estate industry? Here are some of the top niche opportunities:

FOR SALE BY OWNER	BUILDERS	REFERRALS	PAST CLIENT	EXPIRED
REAL ESTATE OWNED	FIRST TIME BUYER	DOWNSIZING	SHORT SALES	
INVESTORS	ONLINE LEADS	PROBATES	JUST SOLD-JUST LISTED	
OPEN HOUSES	DIRECT MAIL	NEIGHBORHOOD FARM	LUXURY PROPERTIES	
ACTIVE LISTING	ACTIVE BUYER	COMMERCIAL	FORECLOSURES	

Look at the diversity in just those listed above. You've heard the expression "jack of all trades, master of none." That's what happens when you attempt to be all things to all people. You can be competent, but your efforts will be so scattered that you will have a hard time creating much success. Creating about four niche areas to focus your efforts on will allow you to become extremely targeted in servicing those niches expertly.

To determine the best niches for you, look at your strengths and weaknesses that we already discussed. Also look at the market trends in your area and examine the need. Ask yourself what you are most passionate about and what you love the most. Get to know other real estate agents around your area and understand their niches. Find areas where there are opportunities to differentiate yourself and also fill some gaps. Doing this will help you settle on what is right for you.

There are some niches that fit everyone's personality: just sold/just listed, open houses, and direct mail, for example. You can approach these tailored to your style, but these are niches everyone can easily work. I recommend you determine four niche areas to work. Mine were FSBOs, Expireds, direct mail, and past client/referrals. This will diversify you enough but keep you focused on becoming an expert in a few areas. Build systems that cater to your niches and implement them. Market specifically to the niche instead of doing generic marketing. Dominate your niche. Initially take them one at a time and work that niche until you've dominated it and are getting consistent results from your efforts. Then take the next one until you've dominated all four niches.

HOW TO OWN AND DOMINATE YOUR NICHE

There are seven steps to owning and dominating your niche. If you follow these steps, you will become an expert and authority in that niche, and you will see your results skyrocket. The seven steps are

1. Determine your four niches (target markets).

2. Attract (lead magnets).

3. Capture leads (landing pages).

4. Cultivate (educate and nurture).

5. Convert (make an offer).

6. Over deliver (customer experience).

7. Capitalize (ascension and retention).

1. Determine your four niches (target markets). We discussed this above. The key is to understand your strengths and weaknesses, and work to your strengths. You also want to know the needs in your market so you choose a niche that is valuable to your area. Then go towards those areas you are passionate about and where you have strengths.

2. Attract (lead magnets). You need to attract prospects, and you're going to do that by using lead magnets. Ask yourself what would attract the person in your first niche to you. What are magnets you can use to attract these people? To dominate a niche, you need things that are bait, and things that the people in your niche can't resist. For example, if you're going after FSBOs, use things like free reports, webinars, and a how-to guide for selling your home. Why? Because it positions you as the expert at the same time it provides value to them.

I want you to focus on becoming a better marketer. In fact, I want you to learn how to become as good of a marketer as you are a salesperson. I want you to stack your skills. Don't be linear; be deep.

I have a coaching client who I helped identify a niche market. He

79

created a first-responder niche that included nurses, firefighters, and police officers. Because it is such a targeted group, he was able to create a very customized marketing program specific to them that spoke to their needs, and his business rapidly expanded as a result. This is something that fit his personality, met a market need, and he is passionate about.

3. Capture leads (landing pages). In the current era, it's important to have a way to capture your prospects, send them to a place to get what you promised them, provide the offering, and capture the lead into a CRM system that continues to market to them from day one. The easiest way to do this is to create a landing page. People are accustomed to using technology to get what they need.

4. Cultivate (educate and nurture). Once you capture these leads and give them what you promised, then it is time to cultivate. To dominate a niche, you've got to cultivate. The seed's been planted; now you're going to water, fertilize, nourish, and communicate with the leads. To cultivate is to educate and nurture. Create drip campaigns and aggressive follow-up that market specifically to your niche.

5. Convert (make an offer). Once you cultivate, you can convert. You can sometimes convert without cultivating, because some people will take action right now. However, the bulk of your prospects are not going to be ready right now, and you're going to have to cultivate that relationship and position yourself as the expert before you make an offer to them.

6. Over deliver (customer experience). Part of differentiating yourself is to over deliver in your customer experience. Don't just do what is expected. Set yourself apart and go the extra mile. Let the customer know you're working for their business. Earn it. Over deliver and create a customer experience that will be remembered when it is time for them to commit, and they will choose you.

7. Capitalize (ascension and retention). I want you to take that focus and realize you've got to capitalize on this opportunity. You do this by ascension and retention. Here's what I mean by that. You generated and converted the lead, listed and sold the house, and you over delivered on customer experience. Now you want to capitalize on the relationship to get repeat referral business and get them to refer you to their friends and family. They now become a Met. The key to building a legacy business is taking care of the people that you did so well in servicing, the people who didn't know you, and that you worked your butt off in converting so the relationship continues on beyond the transaction.

The last thing I want for you is to have a turn 'em and burn 'em operation; that's brutal. That's when you have ticked off customers, no repeat referrals, and people are generally unhappy with you because you just didn't deliver. That is no way to live, and it's no way to serve people. The goal is turn these customers into raving fans.

NICHES: A PERSONAL ILLUSTRATION

I'll wrap up niches with this story. When I was in my early twenties, I went to the Keller Williams' family reunion. That is a convention of about 20,000 Keller Williams Realtors in Las Vegas. It's huge. I was with my mentor, who was high in the company, and he took me under his wing. After the convention, we were going to fly to his $5-million log cabin in the mountains, and we were going to mastermind for three additional days—just him and me. This was an incredible opportunity, and I was super excited. I got into the limo, and he says, "We've got to go pick up Mark."

"Mark who?" I asked.

"Mark Willis."

Mark Willis was the CEO of Keller Williams at the time. He had just finished his final speech at the convention, he leaves the stage, and he gets in the limo with us, and I remember thinking, "What did I do to be in this position at this time?"

My mentor introduced me, saying, "Hey, Mark, this is Hoss. Hoss is dominating listings in our market, he's a go-getter and a hustler, he's got such a bright future ahead of him, and he's a high D and high I. What is your advice to him knowing what you know?"

Mark asked, "What's higher, your D or your I?"

I told him it was my D.

"You're going to get bored," he said, "and you're going to get impatient. You're going to get tired of doing the same thing over and over and over again. You're going to always think that's there's something better that you should be doing. You're going to always want to be moving on to the next thing. That's the weakness of a D, but your strength is the ability to go do those things. If you want to be the most successful you can possibly be, fall in love with the boredom. Fall in love with being bored. Fall in love with what's next. Do it, and do it again and again and again; love it, don't get bored, and then do it again. If you do that, your success will be up to you, and you will be living up to the highest of your potential and your ability. But you're never going to get where you want to be by being impatient and moving on to the next thing, just like everybody else."

> THE FEW WHO DO
> ARE THE ENVY OF
> MANY WHO ONLY
> WATCH.
>
> –JIM ROHN

That's all he said, and it has stuck with me ever since. I want you to realize what your strengths are, what your weaknesses are, who you serve best based on those factors, and know how to strengthen your weaknesses. Know that everything you want to achieve can and will happen, but it will take you sticking to it and having the stick-to-itiveness to not let anything get in between you and success.

☞ ACTIONS TO TAKE

1. Know your DISC personality style by taking the DISC personality test.
2. Identify your four niches.
3. Create a strategy and dominate your niches.

 # KEYS TO SUCCESS

1. Your business can't be all things to all people to excel at anything.
2. Understand your personality style to better understand your strengths and weaknesses.
3. Just because you can do something doesn't mean you should. Trying to be great at too many things simultaneously will not allow you to master any of them, and chances are you will be mediocre as a whole.
4. There are seven steps to owning and dominating your niche.
   1. Determine your four niches (target markets).
   2. Attract (lead magnets).
   3. Capture leads (landing pages).
   4. Cultivate (educate and nurture).
   5. Convert (make an offer).
   6. Over deliver (customer experience).
   7. Capitalize (ascension and retention).

5. Master Lead Conversion

The confidence that you need is belief in your potential.
If you see world class potential in yourself, you'll put forth the effort.
If you don't see the potential, then you won't put forth
the effort and you'll wait for the performance,
and the performance always follows the belief in self.
—Denis Waitley

L ead Conversion is actually one of my favorite subjects because this is the stuff that's going to pay you the rest of your life. As my dad always told me, "If you can sell, you'll never be broke." Once you understand what makes people tick—what gets them to say yes— you have a formula for getting results. Some of the things I'm sharing in this book are things that you have to adjust to over time with market changes. Not these strategies. These are fundamentals; they don't just evaporate with every shifting market. These strategies deal with the human mind and how it works, and implementing these strategies will allow you to differentiate yourself from your competition.

Before we get started with the strategies, it all begins with belief. If you don't really believe in your ability to convert leads, it's not going to happen. If you don't believe that people want to talk to you, and you don't have the skill sets to get them to say yes, then you will find enough things out there to reinforce that belief, and you will find other things to occupy your time to shy away from prospecting in general. So my goal is in this chapter is to give you strategies to make you more confident. I want you to expect results instead of simply waiting for results to come to you. And I want you to do it in a mindset where you are literally having fun!

We're going to get into the psychology of selling and how to get people into a dialogue instantly. This chapter will take some of you outside of your comfort zone. Let it happen. Your comfort zone is what has you exactly where you are right now, and no matter where that is, there's another level for you. You can't continue to get to the next level and the next by doing the same things that got you where you are. What got you to where you are will not get you to where you want to be.

THE FOUR STRATEGIES OF LEAD CONVERSION

Here are the four powerful strategies that when mastered will allow you to significantly increase your leads into conversions:

1. Develop pattern interrupts.

2. Dig deeper.

3. Use voice control.

4. Be direct.

I am going to break each of these down for you, but before I do, I want to encourage you to record your calls, at least for a time. This can be painful in the beginning, but if you have the mindset that this is what will make you better, you will get through it. Listening to your calls will tell you what's working and where you need to continue to improve until it all becomes habit. This is where everything will begin to change for you for the better.

STRATEGY 1: PATTERN INTERRUPT

The first strategy to focus on for lead conversion in order to get people into a dialogue is simply interrupt their pattern. The best way to explain pattern interrupt is to give you an example. Think about getting a phone call at 8:00 p.m. from an 800 number. I know you've had this happen lots of times. The phone rings, and the first thing you think is, "Oh great, it's a telemarketer." Let's just say you decide to answer it, even if your intention is to have them take you off their call list. The telemarketer says, "Hi, is Mr. Pratt in please?" In many cases, they even mispronounce your name. When that happens, what's the first thought that comes to your mind? You want to just hang up, don't you? Why? Well, it's a telemarketer and they're trying to sell you something. Even though you don't know what they're even selling at this point, your first thought is to just hang up.

Your first reaction is to hang up because it's the pattern you've established based on your current mindset and experience. Now let's flip this example into your world. You're prospecting, and you are calling on your expired listings prospects. The prospect answers, and you say, "Hi, Mr. Expired. How are you today?" What do you think their first thought is? They want to hang up. It isn't personal; it is just their pattern. To get them to react differently, you need to create a pattern interrupt.

Let me reiterate this ... *rejection is not personal.* I know it feels personal, but it's not. Prospects are not rejecting *you*; they're rejecting the idea. It is the same way for you with the telemarketer. You aren't rejecting the person—you don't even know them. You don't even know what he's selling. Just like you, they're just rejecting the idea. It's simply their pattern.

To interrupt a prospect's pattern and natural tendency to reject, we have to take away some of their opportunities to reject. How do you do that? First of all, don't ask them how they are today. It gives them an opportunity to reject you. In fact, it isn't just giving them an opportunity, it's setting them up. For an expired listing, you know you aren't the only one who is calling the lead, and the prospect may have gotten what seems like to them 100 calls already today, and if you do and say the same thing that everyone else has, their natural reaction is to want to hang up.

Before getting into the specifics of the pattern interrupt, think about the outcome you want, and have the right mindset. You have to expect to get your prospects into dialogue. Expect to get people to open up and see you differently than they do every one of your competitors who are all calling and saying similar things. To get them into a dialogue, you have to engage them. When you have the right mindset, you then need to be strategic on how to make that happen, and break the prospect's natural response of rejection.

Here's how you're going to break the pattern. Instead of beginning the conversation with pleasantries and leaving yourself open for their dread and rejection, engage them by asking a question. Instead of asking how they are today or if they have a minute to talk, get them legitimately involved in the conversation with something they care about. Approach the conversation like this, "Hey Mr. Expired, it's Hoss Pratt at XYZ Realty. I noticed that your home came up on the MLS as an expired listing today. Why did that property not sell?" See the difference? "Why did that property not sell?" Now you've touched on their pain, and they want to talk to you instead of hanging up. You have broken the pattern.

Let me give you another example. You have an opportunity to meet with a seller that you know will be interviewing four top agents in the area to relist, and you're one of those agents. Before going to the appointment, determine your strategy for why they would want to list with you. If you leave it to chance or just hope that they will like you or your experience the best, then you've just given yourself a 25% chance of getting that listing—every agent there will have credentials.

Your big opportunity is to do the unexpected. If you do the unexpected, they have to think differently. Instead of going in talking about you and why they should hire you, separate yourself from your competition: use the power of persuasion and interrupt their thinking. These principles address the way that people react and make decisions. Using them strategically will help you get people to choose you when making those decisions.

LAWS OF INFLUENCE AND PERSUASION

Law of Authority - people want to follow experts; establish yourself as a true authority in order to gain respect and trust.

Law of Scarcity - people want what they can't have; the less there is available of something, the more people want it.

Law of Reciprocity - the need to reciprocate; people feel indebted to those who do something for them (this can be a small gift, a report, a hand-written note, a special consideration, a referral, etc.).

Law of Social Proof - people want to do what other people are doing. If you have worked with someone else they know, use that to your advantage. If it isn't someone they know specifically, use examples of things that matter to them where they will say, "I want that too."

Law of Commitment and Consistency - people are more likely to follow through when they have agreed to something either verbally or in writing.

Law of Liking - people prefer to say yes to people they know and like.

Let's now go back to your listing appointment. How do you increase your chance beyond 25% of gaining the business, because if all you have is a 25% chance to close, that does not make you want to get out there and prospect. Instead, let me give you an example using the Law of Scarcity.

"Mr. Seller, there's a good chance that we may or may not do business together, because I do turn down more listings than I take. But I promise you this ... at the end of this appointment, you're going to be more educated on the process so you can make a more logical decision on where you want to go from here. I know you will agree with me that the last thing you want is for your listing to expire, right? We both understand the importance of hiring the right real estate agent for you this time around."

What goes through the prospect's mind now? Because people want what they can't have, they're thinking, "Why would you not want to list my home? You're a real estate agent. I've got brand-new granite counter tops, hardwood floors, and you work on commission. Of course you want to list my home." They are convincing themselves why they should list their home with you and how to bring you to that same conclusion.

Using the Law of Scarcity, I was able to completely shift the conversation and cause a pattern interrupt away from the prospect taking an automatic defensive position against whatever I was going to say. I separated myself from the competition simply by doing something different, but I did it in a strategic way that made them want to know more about me and what I'm offering.

Let me give you another example of the Law of Authority. You have a lead for a short sell. The last thing you want to do is what most other agents will do—pour salt on their wound. They would lead into the conversation with something like, "Hey, Mr. Jones, I know you're behind on your mortgage payments; are you familiar with short sells?" That will likely send the prospect's defenses through the roof. Using the Law of Authority, try starting the conversation like this: "Mr. Jones, I'm Hoss Pratt, and I've recently sold a considerable number of homes in your area." Then establish your authority. "I have a quick question for you. I know this call is going to be totally random, but I've got a buyer that's looking to buy a property in your area, and your property matches their criteria perfectly; would you ever consider selling your property for the right price?" What a different approach! This approach comes from a level of contribution—bringing something to the table instead of just taking—and that breaks a pattern that's going to get them to open up and talk to you.

Converting leads is all about influence and persuasion. I challenge you learn more about the Laws of Influence and continue to find ways to use them in your sales conversations so you can create true two-way dialogue with your prospects that will give you the right information to help persuade them to make a decision to hire you. This will give you the advantage every time.

To sum up our first strategy, it is all about pattern interrupt. When you get a prospect on the phone or you are in front of them in person, they have to see you as a different agent within the first few seconds. When you take them off their natural defensive position, you have the opportunity to gain their business.

STRATEGY 2: DIG DEEPER

The second strategy for converting leads more successfully is digging deeper. Digging deeper begins with asking more questions. This is how you're going to get people into a meaningful dialogue. If you think about it, the best salespeople could almost be psychologists because they are so good at getting people to open up by asking the best questions. The same is true with real estate agents. Asking the right questions is the key.

What you want to do is dig deep. When you think about digging deeper, think about the roots of a tree. The deeper the roots, the better the foundation.

Here is an example of how a call might go. "Mrs. Smith, I see your real estate listing has expired. Let me ask you, why did that property not sell?" There are many potential answers, but let's say they tell you that they believe it is because the last agent didn't do enough to market the property. Your next question is going to be asked based on that answer. "What could the last agent have done differently to market the property?" After contemplating, their reply was that he could have held open houses. Do you see how this process is uncovering their pain? "Why are open house important to you?" They answer that they believe open houses would have sold the property, but it isn't the case. In fact, the prospect doesn't really want open houses. What they want is an aggressive agent who will actively market their property. People don't want to wash their face; they just want the acne gone.

By digging deeper, you can find out what their pain is and where they believe the problem was for why their house did not sell the first time around. A lot of people struggle with what questions to ask. The reality is, if you are really listening, the prospect will tell you what questions to ask based on their answers. If you aren't asking the right questions to uncover their pain, how do you know what solutions to offer them? The goal is simply to lead the prospect to self-discover their pain so you can offer the proper solutions.

We will talk about the marketing arsenal in more depth in the next chapter, but having a marketing arsenal at your disposal is critical because that's where you find your solutions. When the prospect says that the last agent didn't do anything to market the property, your response should be: "I understand, Mrs. Jones, the last agent didn't do anything to market the property; that's why we offer our clients an 89-point marketing plan. It is designed to get properties sold the fastest way for the most amount of money."

If the prospect tells you the last agent locked them into a contract, your response should be: "I understand the last agent locked you into a contract; that's why we offer our clients an easy exit listing." You want to find the pain and provide the solution to the pain. If you do that, you're going to give that prospects a good vibe, and you will earn their trust and respect.

Whether you are on the phone or face-to-face, practice this principle. It works for every situation. Practice it in your personal interactions as well. Ask questions based on the answers you receive and see how far that conversation goes. You will be communicating on a level that you've never communicated on before, and your conversations will be more meaningful.

STOP thinking about what you're going to say next, because it gives them the vibe that you're not listening and that you don't care anyway. START providing the solutions to their pain; you already have the solutions, but if you start spouting off solutions before you know what their pain is, you will most likely just be communicating things they don't really care about that much. Keep on point and listen. When responding, be direct. Being direct displays confidence, and confidence is the one trait that every successful salesperson must exhibit. Confident people come from that level of authority we talked about earlier in this chapter. Provide only those solutions that are an answer to their pain. Give them the validation to choose you.

STRATEGY 3: VOICE CONTROL

The third strategy for closing deals is voice control. This is as important as any strategy for lead conversion because how you say it is just as important as what you say. Unfortunately, oftentimes when you are on the phone or in person, you go into "professional" mode and leave out your natural personality and enthusiasm. That may come across as professional, but it is also boring, and it does not "move" the prospect. To engage the prospect and get them to open up, you need to be excited about what you're doing. Enthusiasm is contagious and sells like no other. Enthusiasm also obviously comes from believing in what you sell. If you believe in what you sell, you can't help but be excited about it.

When you're on the phone, the way to get engagement is through your voice. The more engaged you get your prospect, the more they open up to you. So what are some tricks to using good voice control?

If you're not normally an enthusiastic and excited person, try talking fast and loud. Stand up and talk from your gut instead of your throat. Talk with more power, it will create energy and it will carry through the phone lines. Have you ever been on the phone and you can "feel" someone smile? Well, it's true. Be sure to smile on the phone when you're talking. Move your hands. Enunciate your power words. Doing all these little things will create curiosity, and will make people feel like they've had a genuine interaction.

Voice control is the one thing that most everybody leaves out, and it's important. If you aren't creating enthusiasm, excitement, and curiosity then you aren't differentiating yourself from others. This is especially true when you are on the phone, people need to *feel* you.

STRATEGY 4: BE DIRECT

Now let's delve into our fourth strategy for lead conversion. This can be a game-changer, but it could also be the least comfortable for you at the beginning. Keep an open mind.

It all boils down to being more direct. It is critical to be more direct with your prospects because if they don't see you as an authority, you're not going to convert them—it's as simple as that. Sometimes you've got to give your prospects a wake-up call. You have to define what you stand for, and fight for it! No matter what!

If somebody disagrees with you, you have permission to be direct to fight for what you believe. If somebody says, "All you agents are the same," you should take offense to that and tell them so. In response, tell them, "With all due respect, Mr. Seller, that's why your listing expired, because most agents are the same, but I'm not. And here's why I'm not the same as the average agent. Because I focus on selling properties that other agents failed to sell. I sell homes twice as fast as the average agent. The reason is because I have an 89-point marketing plan that's designed to sell properties just like yours the fastest and for the most amount of money."

Being direct shows confidence and demonstrates that you believe in what you're selling. And because you believe in what you're selling, you will fight for what you believe in. You will fight for your value, you will fight for your services, and sometimes you have to be direct and bold with somebody to convince them that they should believe what you believe. Being direct means coming from that high level of authority and radiating confidence so the prospect can't help but pay attention.

Why is being direct so important? People don't typically take action if they're not uncomfortable. When I'm in a conversation with a prospect where I feel I need to be more direct, I will often say some-thing like: "Mr. Seller, can I be direct with you? What you're trying to accomplish isn't going to happen. It's not reality." It is my job to be the authority and tell them like it is, even if it makes them uncomfortable. That's your job, too, as their potential agent.

Think about the last time you were in a listing presentation, and the seller wanted to price their home at $50,000 above market value. What did you tell them? I hope you told them the truth. What you should do is be direct with them.

"Mr. Expired, can I be direct with you? What you're trying to accomplish isn't going to happen. And even if I do sell the property, which I could potentially do because my 89-point marketing plan does work magic in getting properties sold, the property isn't going to appraise for that value anyway. We're all going to be wasting our time, because the deal is going to fall apart before we

> SUCCESS IS SIMPLY A CHOICE. IT'S DOING THE SAME THING OVER AND OVER AND OVER AGAIN UNTIL IT BECOMES MASTERY.

get to the closing table." You have to focus on being more direct with your prospects. You owe it to them to use your expertise and authority to represent them properly.

Practice in advance how to address potential objections so you are prepared to be direct. It comes more naturally to some people than others, but anyone can master this technique with practice and repeti-tion. Success is simply a choice. It's doing the same thing over and over and over again until it becomes a skill. It's getting to that next level. Once you get to that level, you're going to see a huge difference. You're going to radiate confidence.

CREATE AN ALTER EGO

I'm going to teach you a trick that I've used to master these four strategies and stay consistent. Sales is a mind game. We all battle with a plethora of excuses for why we can't focus on prospecting. We reason with ourselves as to why it isn't the right time for the prospect or that we are too busy with other priorities. There are at least 100 excuses to procrastinate instead of focusing on leads. Even when we remove obstacles, it can be one of the most unnatural things some agents do; but in real estate, you don't make money if you don't convert leads. Period. And if you want to make more money, you have to convert more leads.

I want to teach you a trick that will allow you to be the best you possible every day, because my own personal philosophy and creed for myself is to be the best Hoss Pratt I can be every day. And if I'm the best Hoss Pratt that I can be every single day, the rest is history. I want that for you too.

I've picked this up from some of our superstar entertainers. What is a superstar? They are the people that perform far above everybody else in their markets (or their competition). Some of the top entertainers have used this trick, so I decided to use it for certain areas of my life. For our purposes here, let's talk about an alter ego specifically for lead generation. Stay with me … I haven't gone completely crazy.

Have you ever heard of Sasha Fierce in the entertainment world? Sasha Fierce is Beyoncé's alter ego and stage name. Beyoncé has told her story many times about how she's a shy person in general. She has stage fright and can get petrified when thinking about a performance. If you've seen Beyoncé on stage, this may be a surprise to you, because she is an exceptional performer—one of the best in the business. She electrifies and captivates her audiences. How does she overcome her stage fright? The minute she steps foot onto the stage, she goes into this character that she created to be her alter ego—one that is confident, bold, and fierce—Sasha Fierce. That's who we see on stage performing.

What about Clark Kent? Clark Kent is a humble, introverted reporter who hides behind his glasses and his stories and tries to be invisible. He is shy around women and has a manner that is passive and conservative. He is typically described as mild-mannered and he wears bland, neutral-colored clothing. Enter Superman, his alter ego!

Clark Kent transitions into Superman to fight crime and stand up for the little guy. He is bold and confident and the complete opposite of Clark Kent.

Another great example is Eminem. Eminem is one of the greatest hip-hop/rap artists that has ever existed. He has amazing talents. He has had 10 number one albums on the Billboard charts, sold more than 90 million albums worldwide, won 13 Grammy awards, and was the first rap artists to win an Academy Award for Best Original Song for "Lose Yourself" for the movie *8 Mile*. I'm a fan, and we were actually born in the same town. Marshall Mathers is his given name. Eminem is his alter ego when performing. Even Eminem has an alter ego called Slim Shady. He has multiple alter egos he steps into depending on what he's doing, how he's performing, and where he's performing. He's a multi-dimensional talent.

Creating an alter ego allows a transformation from your comfort zone into the best version of you. Your alter ego is fearless and is good at everything you're bad at or uncomfortable with. Just because you're bad at something now doesn't mean you have to stay bad. Remember, mindset is 99% of success. So create an alter ego and put that alter ego on the phone. If you're not good, then don't put "you" on the phone. Go into character. I know it will take some getting used to, but you can do it, and when you completely let go you will get better at selling. Zig Ziglar says, "Timid people have skinny kids." I dare you to be bold.

For myself, I developed a trigger. My trigger was that every day when I got on the phone to prospect, I put on a white Nike golf glove. This white Nike golf glove had holes in it. It was all from dialing for dollars and smiling and dialing. When that white Nike golf glove went on, I was a different person. I turned it on; it was as if I just put my Superman outfit on. I was no longer battling fear because my alter ego was fearless.

Create that character for yourself. Create a character that is good at everything you're not great at so you don't have to deal with your mindset and your fears consistently on a daily basis. I tell my coaching clients this all the time. I don't want you on the phone; I want you to put your alter ego on the phone so you don't have to deal with all the emotions. It's amazing what happens in your mind when you create a trigger to shift the mindset. Who will your alter ego be? Have fun with it. This is one of the best things that I've taught my clients to do and that I've done in my own business that is a totally outside-the-box, wacky, crazy idea. But I guarantee you this—it works like magic. Everyone already has different roles they play in life, and each of those roles acts differently in specific settings. Create characters for these roles, and you'll create bigger success.

ACTIONS TO TAKE

1. Study the Laws of Influence and Persuasion.
2. Record your calls so you can become better and better at converting leads (where legal).
3. Ask more questions. Practice digging deeper both in your business and your personal conversations.
4. Create an alter ego.

KEYS TO SUCCESS

1. If you don't really believe in your ability to convert leads, it's not going to happen.
2. There are four powerful strategies that when mastered will allow you to significantly increase your leads into conversions:
    a. Develop pattern interrupts.
    b. Dig deeper.
    c. Use voice control.
    d. Create an alter ego.
3. Rejection is not personal. Prospects are not rejecting you; they are rejecting an idea.
4. Understanding and utilizing the Laws of Influence and Persuasion will dramatically increase your lead conversions.
5. Dig deeper by asking the right questions; listen to the answers to uncover the prospect's pain; and provide the solution to those pains. Be direct and position yourself as an authority.

6. Voice control is as important as any lead conversion strategy because how you say it is just as important as what you say.

7. Being direct is a key lead conversion strategy because people don't take action until they are uncomfortable. Establish yourself as the authority by being direct.

8. Success is simply a choice. It's doing the same thing over and over and over again until it becomes a skill.

9. Creating an alter ego allows a transformation from your comfort zone into the best version of you.

6. Deploy a Marketing Arsenal

*The key is to set realistic customer expectations,
and then not to just meet them, but to exceed them—
preferably in unexpected and helpful ways.*
—RICHARD BRANSON

D o you know the answer to this question: "Why should I hire you over your competitor"? It's something prospects often ask. Real estate agents are a dime a dozen. Everybody and their mom has a real estate license, so why should they use you?

WHAT MAKES YOU DIFFERENT?

I'm on the road conducting seminars the majority of the year. I'm in front of hundreds of agents every week, and when I ask that question, I always hear the same answer. They say things like, "I'm honest; I'm loyal and trustworthy; I've been doing this for over 10 years; I have these credentials; Everything I touch turns to sold; I'm a house-sold name." There are two problems with this: (1) if they all say the same thing, this is what makes them the same, not what makes them different; and most importantly, (2) it's all about THEM. What do people care about? They care about themselves, their time, and their money.

In order to convert your prospects and differentiate yourself from your customers, you need to have a marketing arsenal. This arsenal should contain all the support materials that define why your prospect should choose you—things they care about—and that will help save them time and money. It is paramount to your success. I'm going to give you some proven things that will do this, and when you implement this arsenal, you will be able to separate yourself from your competition and grow your business.

In chapter 2 we talked about developing a top-producing mindset, and I gave you this statistic: 95% of the transactions done in most markets are done by 5% of the agents. This means you have 5% of the agents doing 95% of the deals. Do you think these 5% are separating themselves from the pack by doing the same things as the other 95%? No, of course not. I would ask you then to get in the right mindset and be open to changing your thinking on what it will take for prospects to choose you because of the value and differentiation you provide. I'm going to give you the tools. You just have to embrace them and utilize them.

This chapter is NOT about real estate; it is about marketing. You are a marketer who just happens to sell real estate. You want to be in the 5%, and in being in the 5% you've got to have a clearly defined plan on why people should use you over your competitors.

Every seller has a pain, and you've got to be able to provide the solution to that pain. We touched on this previously. Here are some common pains sellers have when selling a property:

- They want to sell their property fast.
- They can't afford your commission, so they'd prefer to sell it on their own and save money.
- The last agent did not market their home.
- The previous agent did not communicate with them.
- They don't want to be locked into a contract.

All these objections—or pains—are things you hear every single day, and I can help you overcome these by simply showing you how to help your sellers—how you can solve their problems. That's why you need a marketing arsenal. It provides the solution to the pain, not you. Remember, this is not about you. You need to give them tangible programs and systems that provide these solutions.

IF YOUR PROSPECT SEES YOU AS A PROVIDER OF SOLUTIONS, YOU WILL HAVE DIFFERENTIATED YOURSELF FROM OTHER AGENTS, AND YOUR BUSINESS WILL GROW.

If your prospect sees you as a provider of solutions, you will have differentiated yourself from other agents, and your business will grow. Let's build your marketing arsenal.

You will want to have many things in your marketing arsenal, but what I want to focus on in this book are things that will help you differentiate yourself. There are five critical parts to your arsenal that will help you overcome most every pain your prospect has in selling their home, and they are 100% focused on *them*. These five are

1. **Performance Guarantee**. Simply put, this guarantees your performance; if you don't do what you say you will do within a certain period of time, you will do X.

2. **Easy Exit Listing**. People don't like being locked into a contract, and this takes all the risk (and therefore pain) out of hiring you. Make it risk-free for your prospects to use you.

3. **89-Point Marketing Plan**. Showing you have an aggressive, comprehensive plan to sell their home fast gives them the confidence that you can do what you say you can do.

4. **Smart Seller Program**. This program allows them to sell the home themselves while you carry the listing; if they procure the buyer, they don't pay commission.

5. **Communication Guarantee**. This is a guarantee that you will call them on a specific day every week or they can fire you.

6. **Certified Pre-Owned Program.** It's a known fact that the "Seal of Approval" stamp increases desirability and sales with ANY product or service.

By offering these five components of the marketing arsenal, this is going to put your ability to convert leads on steroids. Having this arsenal will allow you to change the dialogue you have with your prospects. By providing solutions to their pains, they are going to open up to you. By sharing with them the things they care about and the benefits of your offerings, you will be able to separate yourself from your competition. They will see you as an authority, and you will be more confident.

1. PERFORMANCE GUARANTEE

Your performance guarantee is the single most important piece of your marketing arsenal. You can dominate any market without knowing a soul in it by having a performance guarantee. Within the first 12 months, you can be a top 1% agent in that market simply because you have a better performance guarantee that shows people what you do differently.

Let me explain what the performance guarantee is. It guarantees your performance; sounds simple, right? It guarantees to your prospect that you will do what you say you will do, or they can fire you. You have to decide for yourself what your guarantees will be, but here are some of the best ones that are working in today's market that set a time limit for selling:

• I will sell your home in 39 days, or I'll sell it for free.

• I will sell your home in 39 days, or you can fire me (even though it is not the most aggressive guarantee, this is a good one for somebody who doesn't want to take a lot of risk).

• I will sell your home guaranteed, or I'll buy it. (This is a great guarantee to find investment opportunities.)

Another type of performance guarantee is the "I'll buy it" guarantee. Don't freak out about that one until you know what I'm talking about. I'm going to walk you through this and explain to you in layman's terms exactly what is involved, how to protect yourself, and how to bring value to your prospects by offering them this type of performance guarantee.

What postcard do you think would get a better response: one with your 1990 Glamour Shot that says the equivalent of, "I'm a houseSold name and everything I touch turns to sold," or one that said, "Your home sold in 39 days guaranteed or I'll pay your mortgage until it sells?"

On the other hand, whenever you're going after your Met database, you can brand your name and your face all day long because these people already know you, like you, love you, and trust you. You don't have to bring in your performance guarantee to that market. You want to tailor your performance guarantee to the "Haven't Met" market, because that's what is going to get them to respond. Once they respond and you meet them, they like you and trust you, and then you can brand your name and your face all day long to them. Hopefully, that makes sense because so many people overthink and overanalyze this concept. The reality is it's a call to action—a hook—to get people to respond.

I moved to Dallas from Missouri in my early twenties in a market where I didn't know anybody. In my first six months in real estate I did not take one listing. In fact, I blew $50,000. Six months into my first year, I implemented a performance guarantee. My performance guarantee was, "Your home sold in 39 days or I'll sell it for free." From the day I implemented that performance guarantee until 30 days later, I had 30 signs in the ground. I got 30 listings in 30 days. The second month I did the same thing, and the pattern continued. The first six months I spent branding my name and my face, but it wasn't until I started branding my performance guarantee when everything changed for me. I am so passionate about this because it literally changed my life, and I look at other agents across the country and I see them have the exact same results. I want the same results for you.

When determining your specific performance guarantee, use an aggressive number of days. Use a number you're comfortable with but not *too* comfortable. It also needs to be a number that the seller will think is aggressive and will motivate you to focus on getting their property sold. Whatever number you choose, the number should end in a 7 or a 9. Psychologically, 99 cents seems like a lot less than a dollar. Giving a 37-day guarantee seems like it is a lot less than 40.

I was watching TV recently, and I want to share this advertisement with you because it struck home. It was a commercial for Jos. A. Bank. You've probably seen this commercial, because they've been running it for at least a few years. They offer a "Buy 1 suit, get 3 suits free—this Saturday only promotion." Jos. A. Banks has been in business almost as long as every other men's clothing company on the planet. Why are they not running ads that say, "We've been in business since 1905, we're family owned, and you can trust our quality"? That's image advertising; it doesn't work. When they run the "Buy 1 suit, get 3 suits free—this Saturday only deal," why do you think that it works? It's a call to action. It's limited availability (it's scarcity). And the ad focuses on what the consumer wants.

Let's talk about restrictions for the performance guarantee. One restriction that you may want to add is that the seller must have the home professionally staged up front by a licensed home stager. You can explain to the seller that if you're going to guarantee selling their property in 39 days and risk giving up your commission, you want this property to show like a model home. It's a fact that a home that's staged sells much faster than a house that's not.

Another possible restriction would be to require the seller to hire a licensed appraiser to appraise the property. In order to determine the home is priced at market value, an appraisal will allow the home to qualify for the performance guarantee. Some people require the seller to have a licensed real estate inspector inspect the property, and then fix the agreed-upon items that come back on the inspection report in order to qualify for the guarantee.

You may want to restrict your guarantee to listings within a certain price range—perhaps between $150,000 and $500,000. You would want to offer this restriction if you're using a more aggressive performance guarantee. You may also want to require an agreement on pre-determined price reductions. I think this is fantastic whether you use it in a performance guarantee or not. Customize your own guarantee, but include it in your arsenal.

Personally, I used the free guarantee where I guaranteed to sell it for free if I didn't sell the property within 39 days. I had three restrictions: (1) the seller had to have the home appraised up front by a licensed appraiser, then price the property at a predetermined price; (2) the seller had to have the home inspected by a licensed inspector, and then the seller would fix everything on the inspection report, because if I'm going to waive my commission, the property's got to be sound; and (3) they had to have the home professionally staged upfront. Those were my three restrictions.

To present this to the prospect, I would just say, "Mrs. Jones, if you will have the home appraised, inspected, and staged, it is going to take about $1,400 out-of-pocket. If you do that and I don't sell the property in 39 days, I'll waive my commission. But let me ask you a quick question. Is it worth the wait if I can get an extra $30,000-$40,000 but it took me an extra 60 days to sell the house?" Most people don't end up wanting the performance guarantee—they want more money. But the offer of a performance guarantee got you the appointment and appealed to their pain. If they do take the guarantee, then they have put you in the best possible position to sell the property based on the work done up front.

2. EASY EXIT LISTING

The Easy Exit Listing agreement simply is what it says it is. It allows the prospects the ability to fire you if they're not satisfied with your services. It makes it risk-free for your clients to use you. If a client is not satisfied with your services, they can fire you.

I want you to understand a very important thing. Just because a seller calls you and they are unhappy doesn't mean they really want to fire you. It may mean you didn't do a good enough job communicating with them or you didn't do what you said you were going to do.

Offering an easy exit listing is going to totally separate you from your competition, as that's always your goal. Some people are hesitant to give the seller this type of an "out," but if a seller wants to cancel a listing, chances are you're going to cancel it anyway. Nobody wants to work with someone that doesn't want them. Give them an easy exit.

If a seller says they don't want to be locked into a contract, here's how you can sell the Easy Exit Listing: "I understand you don't want to be locked into a contract. That's the reason I offer all of my clients an Easy Exit Listing. If you're not satisfied with our services, you can fire us. It's absolutely risk-free for you to use us."

Implementing the Easy Exit Listing as part of your marketing arsenal will allow you to get face-to-face appointments with your prospects.

3. 89-POINT MARKETING PLAN

Most agents simply don't have a marketing plan; there's nothing that separates them from everybody else, and sellers want an agent who's going to actively market their home. The seller will always hire the agent who's the most aggressive. They're looking for an agent who has the strongest marketing plan and who will bring value to them. This also overcomes the "What are you going to do to market my home?" objection that we hear, or "What do you do different that every other real estate agent?" objection. This 89-Point Marketing Plan is designed to get properties sold the fastest and for the most amount of money.

Your marketing plan is simply going to get you in the door. It's going to show people that you're more aggressive and what you do differently than every other agent out there. Most agents do the same thing; I just simply broke down the process so the perception is something much different and makes the seller believe they have to have it. The main point is that a seller wants to know that you have a plan to market their home to get it sold.

I'm reminded of a story, a story about Herman Cain. Some of you may remember Herman Cain as he was a presidential candidate in the 2012 election. He was previously the CEO of Godfather's Pizza. In the race, America was looking for a leader that would be able to put the economy back on track. Americans wanted a plan.

Right before the debates, Herman Cain came out with his plan called the "999 Plan." He said "My 999 plan is going to get America back on track. My 999 plan is going to get this economy roaring. My 999 plan is going to create more jobs than any other plan." All of a sudden he went from the bottom of the heap to the top because America saw a man with a plan.

4. SMART SELLER PROGRAM

The Smart Seller Program is simply a program that you offer your sellers that's going to allow them to sell the property themselves while it's listed with you. It also comes with a menu of commission rates and a no-hassle presentation. Here's why it's important to implement the smart seller program. This program will drastically separate you from your competition, and it overcomes the "I want to sell the property on my own" objection that we hear so frequently.

This is an especially good program if you're calling on your For Sale By Owner prospects. They love the Smart Seller Program, because it allows them to continue marketing the property. If they sell the property, and they procure the buyer, then it's 0% commission. The seller can market the property through open houses, Craigslist ads, for sale by owner sites, newspapers, or whatever avenue they prefer. The only thing the seller cannot do is put a For Sale By Owner sign in the front yard—your For Sale sign goes in the front yard.

The Smart Seller Program is going to provide the solution to a seller's pain if they want to sell it themselves and save money. The smart seller program allows them to continue doing what they're doing. You want to say something like this to your seller: "Mr. Smith, consider it a race. You're going to market the property through your FSBO sites and open houses; continue doing that, and if you sell the home, you don't owe me anything. The only time you would owe me is if I sell the property. We're both working hard toward the common goal of getting your property sold. It's a win-win."

This program will allow you to set so many more appointments. The better news is that when you take the listing, most often the seller gives up marketing the property themselves.

5. COMMUNICATION GUARANTEE

Question. What is the number one complaint that sellers have of real estate agents? Lack of communication. They don't get enough communication as to what it happening in the sale of their home. That's a reasonable complaint. The seller is paying you a large amount of money to get their home sold, and if they don't know what you're doing, it causes angst.

The Communication Guarantee is a program you offer your sellers that guarantees you will communicate with them. You will guarantee that you're going to call your seller on a specified day of the week. If you fail to call the seller on that day of the week, then the seller can fire you on the spot, no strings attached. You can modify this by offering a dollar amount or a reduction in commissions if you fail to live up to your commitment. There are no restrictions on the communication guarantee because it is 100% about you living up to a commitment. It is completely in your control. If you communicate with your seller every week like you say you're going to then you have nothing to worry about.

How many times have you heard, "My last agent took my listing and I never heard from them again." That's why properties expire. Oftentimes the agent is scared to communicate with their seller because they need to ask for a price reduction or ask the seller to do something they won't want to do. The great thing is that it's going to force you to communicate. This guarantee will force you to talk about feedback from showings, discuss where the market is today, talk about what needs to be done differently to get the property sold, and, obviously, reach your seller's goals.

Once you have your strong communication guarantee, explain to the seller that you plan to call them every Tuesday. Tell them you're going to talk about the good, the bad, and the ugly. Let them know that if you don't call, that means you've either died or won the lottery. Tell them if you die or win the lottery, they can fire you. Doing this will allow you to separate yourself from your competitors.

Remember that a Marketing Arsenal will allow you to be prepared to overcome your prospect's objections by offering them a solution to their pain. In the wise words of the late great Peter Drucker, "The aim of marketing is to know and understand the customer so well that the product or service fits him and sells itself."

6. CERTIFIED PRE-OWNED PROGRAM

One of the solutions that works in any market is the Certified Pre-Owned Program. The Certified Pre-Owned Program attracts more realistic sellers, and it attracts more buyers and real estate agents to your listings. Perhaps even more important is that it adds certainty to the transaction.

One day, I was driving by a Mercedes Benz dealership near my house in Plano, Texas. The sign facing the street said "Certified Pre-Owned Cars." Then I drove by the BMW dealership, because it's on my reticular activator; now I'm paying attention to everywhere I see it, and I'm starting to see all these high-end car dealerships offering Certified Pre-Owned. They're not even calling them used cars. I thought that would be pretty genius if we could apply the same system to real estate. Why not Certified Pre-Owned homes?

111

By nature, real estate sales create uncertainty. When there is uncertainty you have fear and doubt, which brings with it negative emotion. You want to eliminate these emotions to make negotiations easier.

Imagine you have two homes. Home A is $298,000. It's a Certified Pre-Owned home, it comes with a three-year home warranty, a 500 point inspection has been completed and everything on the report has been fixed, the appraisal has been done, and it's passed a pest inspection.

The other home, Home B, is $285,000, and everything is to be negotiated just like all the other transactions that you do, everything is "AS IS." As a real estate agent, which would you rather represent? If you offered that, how do you think other real estate agents would feel about your listings? How do you think the seller would feel about taking away the uncertainty? Listing Certified Pre-Owned homes helps you stand out and gives you an advantage.

☞ ACTIONS TO TAKE

1. Create your own marketing arsenal which will allow you to be prepared to overcome your prospect's objections and offer up solutions for their pain.
2. Give your prospect solutions and programs which allow you to give them what they want and takes out the risk that causes them fear.

♔ KEYS TO SUCCESS

1. If you cannot differentiate yourself from your competitors, there is no reason for a prospect to choose you.
2. If your prospect sees you as a provider of solutions, you will have differentiated yourself from other agents, and your business will grow.
3. Join **Listing Boss Academy**. See my invitation on page 201.

7. Leverage Systems and Tools

When companies fail, or fail to grow, it's almost always because they don't invest in the people, the systems, and the processes they need.
—Howard Schultz, Former Starbucks CEO

A s you can already tell, I'm a believer in allocation of time, money, and resources. There are tools out there that will make your life so much easier and will make you so much more money that you can't afford not to use them. There are many systems and tools available, so I'm just going to share with you the no-brainer ones I believe you must employ to get to the next level faster.

It's incredible to me how many real estate agents don't have systems. They go to the office every day, but they don't know what to do day in and day out. They just go straight to the coffeepot and shoot the breeze (which often goes to negativity). People tend to want to talk about how bad everything is. I highly recommend you just walk straight to your office, shut the door, and stay in your bubble by listening to positive affirmations and music, and looking at positive pictures and quotes.

The reality is, most agents shouldn't even be entrepreneurs, because they run this business more like a hobby. That's why there is such a high turnover rate in this industry. By learning how to use systems, tools, and processes to help you create success in your business, you're going to be on a whole different playing field compared to your competitors. My goal is to help you build a well-oiled machine that is like a water-tight sealed compartment, where no lead will ever fall through the cracks. I want you to have a system in place that tells you what to do every day rather than you trying to figure out what to do like everyone else. I want to give you systems to help manage *you*. I don't want you to manage the systems; I want them to help manage you.

Before I get into the systems, I want to talk to you about some tools, because it's very important to employ tools that make your job easier. I want to tell you a quick story.

When I first moved to Dallas and got into real estate, I went to one of the top agents in the area. I was working hard, but I was struggling. He was a young guy, and I asked him, "What are you doing to go out there and get all those listings?"

"Well," he said, "I'm going after For Sale By Owners and Expireds."

I explained that I was also going after FSBOs, and he asked me how I was getting the leads.

"I'm driving around getting them."

He looked out the window, then looked back at me and said, "Is that your F-350 Ford diesel truck that you just parked in the parking lot?" When I said yes, he started laughing and asked me how much I was spending in fuel each week.

I told him I was spending a lot, but how else was I supposed to get the leads?

He asked, "Well, haven't you heard about FSBO and expired lead providers?"

When I gave him a blank stare and explained that I had not heard about them, he explained that this was a service that sends you the FSBOs and Expireds every day. Remember early in the book when I said that everyone is one piece of information away from achieving any level of success? This was that one thing for me at the time.

The next day I couldn't get to my office fast enough to sign up for one of these services. The following day, I had a listing, and the next day I had another listing. In fact, I ended up taking 30 listings that first month. I went from having zero listings to 30 by doing this one thing. I was literally going broke trying to get on my feet in the industry, and this one tool changed everything for me. And it happened quickly.

I want to stress to you that the principle of having tools and systems is never changing, whether you are small or large business. But as you are beginning to grow your business and you begin putting some of the things in this book to work for you, make sure that you have the internal systems to manage it all. One of the worst things that can happen to you is to grow too fast. Be prepared for the growth and put the right people and technology in place to help you execute.

DEPEND ON A CRM

I get asked this question all the time, "Hoss, what is the best CRM to use?" My answer is simple, it's the CRM that you use. The number one tool that you must have is a good Customer Relationship

Management (CRM) software. What a CRM does is provides a system to manage your contacts. It's amazing how many agents are trying to manage their real estate business on an Excel spreadsheet. I'm here to tell you that you had better step up your game, because it's impossible to grow to the level that you're capable of by managing your contacts and running your business on an Excel spreadsheet or even in Outlook.

Find a CRM provider that will allow you to manage your contact database and allow you to build action plans inside the system. Many have an arsenal of marketing materials like letters, postcards, and emails. Therefore, if you get a call from a sign, you can have an action plan already built in that reminds you to call them every day, or automatically sends them a particular email or marketing piece. The most important part of a CRM that most people do not use utilize is their action plans. I never recommend a CRM that doesn't allow you to build your own action plans, follow-up campaigns, or follow-up sequences.

Think of your CRM as a hub. It's the hub of your operation. This is what tells you what to do, and if you have an assistant, it will tell your assistant what to do. It will be the hub for every team member and tell them what to do. You have to have systems that manage you instead of you managing them. Building action plans into the CRM supports that. Top Producer is the one I used, and they continually innovate and upgrade their technology. Other competitors are following their lead as well, so you have some other solid options.

If you've purchased a CRM before and didn't use it, I encourage you to be open-minded to trying again. This is critical to managing your customers and leads, and having a strong system to manage your activity. You will probably never implement all the things a CRM is capable of, but it is important to use the action plans. This will tell you what to do, when to do it, and how to do it.

USE A GOOD LEAD PROVIDER

Once you get the CRM, you've got to build the system and have the leads to fuel the system. When I'm talking leads, there are so many different lead providers out there, but I'm going to focus on the fastest ways to get listings. The two fastest ways by far are going after For Sale By Owners (FSBOs) and Expireds. These are the lowest hanging fruit in every market. They are already there, and they're holding their hand up saying, "Hey, I want to sell my home!" All you have to do is convince them they need you, and that you have a good marketing arsenal you can deploy.

Whatever lead provider you use, it is critical that they make it easy for you to get the leads. Then you're going to take the leads and put them into your CRM. Next you will deploy the system inside the CRM so it will tell you what to do, when to do it, and how to do it. It's a numbers game, and to be playing the game, I want you to be focused on maximizing those leads.

Be sure to find a lead provider who specializes in whatever your niche market is so you maximize your opportunity. Real estate is a sales business. You are a salesperson. Set yourself up to have a steady flow of qualified leads, and your business will grow if you have a system for properly working and managing those leads. I always tell people, being a broke real estate agent is a choice. You decided to be broke. I've never met an agent that communicated their services to a seller's need every single day who was broke. The only agents that I've ever met who were broke were agents that didn't prospect and lead generate.

INVEST IN AN AUTO DIALER

An auto dialer is a tool that will automatically make your calls for you, so you literally upload your numbers, hit Start, and the system will automatically call through the list. You can automatically leave prerecorded messages, automatically record the conversation, and automatically send an email saying,

AN AUTO DIALER WILL CUT DOWN YOUR PROSPECTING TIME BY AS MUCH AS 75%.

"Hey, I just left you a voicemail; give me a call when you're free."

I'll tell you right now, having an auto dialer is a big deal for maximizing your time. It will cut down your prospecting time by as much as 75%.

DEPLOY SIX ESSENTIAL SYSTEMS

Now that you have the right tools, you want to build the systems. When you get a lead, you have a full system you put it through. The system is automated through your CRM. There are six systems that are essential for growing your business. They are

1. **Lead Daily Action Plan**: Call a lead every day for 30 days.

2. **Lead 3-Day Action Plan**: Call a lead every 3 days for 2 months.

3. **Lead Weekly Action Plan**: Call a lead every week for 6 months.

4. **Lead Biweekly Action Plan**: Call a lead every 2 weeks.

5. **Lead Monthly Action Plan**: Call a lead every month.

6. **Lead Bimonthly Action Plan**: Call a lead every 2 months.

Before you freak out, let me explain all these systems. These systems ensure that every lead is accounted for, and we always know where it is in the system; all we have to do it execute on what the system tells us. Using these systems ensures you have a plan in place to market to your leads consistently and keeps leads from falling through the cracks. You put the leads into the proper system based on the information you gather during your initial conversations. In doing this, you're building a pipeline.

To build a predictable pipeline of leads, all you have to do is do what you say you will do every single day. The Lead Daily Action Plan doesn't really mean you are going to call every day, but it does mean the lead will be in front of you every day. You can then make decisions on a case-by-case basis on what to do with that lead. Keeping the lead in front of you allows you to better understand their motivation.

For example, on an expired list, you are going to call them every day for the first week. If you leave a message you would put LM for "left message" in the notes section of the CRM software. If you called but didn't leave a message, you would indicate DNLM. If there was no answer, you would indicate NA. Take good notes of every single contact attempt. This is where people screw up; they fly by the seat of their pants, and they don't have an organized system. It does you absolutely no good to have leads if you have no follow-up campaigns and systems.

There are two ways you can typically set up an action plan in your CRM. You can enter them from "start day" or from "previous activity was completed." Depending on the system and timing, you will have a series of calls set up for each lead. If you have any trouble setting up your action plans, contact your CRM provider, and they will help you. The key is to use systems to automate the process. If you don't, they will get lost in the shuffle of all the things that need to happen. It won't be consistent, and you won't convert as many leads.

QUIT TALKING ABOUT IT, AND BE ABOUT IT.

If you utilize these systems, your pipeline is going to continue to grow, your call list will continue to grow, your listing inventory will continue to grow, and your bank account is going to continue to grow. The systems will change everything. Duplicate the systems for the buyer side and just change the type of lead.

Having systems is critical to maximizing your opportunities. Let the system manage you and tell you what to do, when to do it, and how to do it. You will never have to worry about being unorganized once you have all these systems deployed. Quit talking about it, and be about it.

 ## ACTIONS TO TAKE

1. Purchase and set up a CRM system.
2. Subscribe to a lead source, and input your leads into your CRM.
3. Invest in an auto dialer.

4. Create your six essential systems and input them into your CRM as action plans.

 ## KEYS TO SUCCESS

1. The number one tool that you must have is a good Customer Relationship Management (CRM) software.
2. Think of your CRM as the hub of your operation. It will tell you what to do, when to do it, and how to do it.
3. Utilize your CRM to automate systems for prospecting.
4. Quit talking about it, and *be* about it.

8. Master Your Listing Presentation

Be so good they can't ignore you.
—STEVE MARTIN

I'll never forget my first listing appointment. I was terrified. It was a referral from my insurance agent. I remember driving to the appointment. My palms were sweaty, sweat was pouring from my forehead, and as I pulled up to the house, I remember thinking, "Okay, God, please let this be easy. Please just let me get this listing." I walked up to the front and knocked. He answered, I shook his hand, and he invited me in to sit at his table.

I looked down and saw a Missouri Tigers coaster on the table. I'm from Missouri, and we're in Texas.

"Oh, Missouri Tigers," I said. "I'm from Missouri."

"Really? What part?"

I told him where I was from, then he shared where he was from, and right then there was a magical moment where we bonded because I found rapport with the seller.

RAPPORT TRUMPS EVERYTHING.

He signed the listing. I didn't even have to do the presentation. He didn't even care. It was literally the easiest, best listing appointment I've ever been on, and it was my first one. I thought they were all going to be that easy. Of course, they weren't, but the lesson that I learned from that was that rapport trumps everything. If you build enough rapport with the seller, you could fail at all the other things, and it can still make all the difference in the world.

APPOINTMENTS 101

Let's first examine what needs to happen before your listing appointment. Before spending the time to conduct the appointment, be sure the prospect has been qualified. Have you determined that the prospect is ready to list their home and that you have a legitimate opportunity to gain the business? The biggest mistake that you can ever make is going on appointments that aren't qualified. Your time is too valuable to be wasting on appointments that you have little or no chance of converting.

Here's how you qualify an appointment: "Mr. Seller, if I come out there and you love everything about me—you love my marketing plan, and we agree on price, terms, and conditions—is there any reason I cannot earn your business at that appointment?" This is an important question to ask, because it will be useful later.

If the seller tells you, "No, I see no problem in listing with you if I like everything I see," and later on says, "Let me think about it. I'll call you tomorrow," you can remind them what they said previously.

> **HAVE YOU DETERMINED THAT THE PROSPECT IS READY TO LIST THEIR HOME AND THAT YOU HAVE A LEGITIMATE OPPORTUNITY TO GAIN THE BUSINESS?**

"Remember on the phone, you said if you loved everything about me, I could earn your business? What is it you didn't see tonight that you are looking for in an agent?"

Make sure to verify in advance that both spouses are going to be at the appointment. You want to remove the potential obstacle of the prospect not listing at the appointment because their spouse is not there. You want to make sure you're the last agent they are interviewing, and the way to do that is to get the listing at the appointment. Otherwise, there is no reason to go on that appointment.

Before your appointment, complete a seller discovery sheet. The seller discovery sheet is a series of questions that gives you the 30,000-foot view of their situation. It gives you perspective. Fill it out as you are communicating with the seller. It will give you valuable information on the seller and their situation prior to going on the appointment. It is a combination of details about the home itself, what they are looking to get from the home, and how motivated they are to sell.

Seller Discovery Sheet

Name:_____ Address being listed:_____

Mailing Address:_____

Home # _____ Work #_____ Cell #_____

Email: _____ 2nd Email: _____

Best Time to Contact _____ Prefer: ☐ Email ☐ Phone

How did you hear about us?   Source 1:_____ Source 2: _____

How many: Bedrooms _____   Bathrooms _____   Square Feet _____   Stories _____
              Garages _____   Living Rooms _____   Dining Areas _____   Fireplace _____
Describe the Lot: _____   Exterior _____   Outbuildings_____
Decks/Patios _____   Sprinkler System _____   Storm Cellar _____
Pool: _____ ☐ Inground ☐ Above   Fenced Yard _____
Are there any covenants, restrictions, home owner dues? _____
What would you say are the best features of the home?
_____   _____
_____   _____

When would you like for this move to happen?_____
Will you be staying in the area or moving away?_____ (If away) Where? _____
Why have you decided to move there? _____
     If Staying here: ☐ Buying ☐ Bought ☐ Renting
     If buying, set up Buyer Specialist to get details. If relocating, offer relocation assistance.
TARGET DATE: _____
Is this your: ☐ Personal Home ☐ Rental   ☐ Occupied ☐ Vacant
When would be a good time for us to come out? _____ Days or Evenings? _____
Is there anyone else involved in the sale of the home? _____ Are they willing to sale? _____
Have you done any upgrades since you purchased the home? _____
Are you aware of any repairs that might need to be done? _____
On a scale of 1 - 10, how would you rate your home? _____
How long have you owned your home? _____ How much did you pay for your home? _____
Have you had a recent appraisal/market analysis? _____ Why? _____
Do you have an idea of what your home will sell for? _____
How did you arrive at that number?_____
Do you know the approx. balance on your mortgage? _____ 2nd Mtg _____
If necessary, are you prepared to bring money to closing?_____ Possible SHORT SALE? _____
On a scale of 1 to 10, how motivated are you to sell your home? _____
What would it take to get you to a 10? _____
Do you plan on interviewing other agents? _____
GREAT!! The reason I ask is because we would like to be last. That way you can see all the different marketing strategies other companies have and compare
with ours. Would that be ok?_____
(If interviewing) I would like you to make a promise to me. We are going to put a lot of time and effort in getting ready for our appointment, please do me a
favor and don't list your home with anyone until you've heard what we have to offer that no one else can, is that okay? Mr. Seller, I want to make you aware
that there are some agents that will do or say anything to get you to SIGN PAPERWORK on their first appointment, especially if they know we are coming out
behind them. Fair enough?
Mr. Seller, one last question. If everything sounds good and the price is acceptable, will you be ready to put your home on the
market when we come out on _____ at _____?

You can download this resource at www.listingboss.com/group

I have included a sample Seller Discovery Sheet here. The next step before going on the appointment is to prepare the numbers. Over the years, most agents have always used a Comparative Market Analysis (CMA), but I want to change your paradigm a little bit because in today's market it is important to start using more specialized reporting tools to provide the numbers. Give them charts, graphs, and statistics so they can see these numbers in real time! There are third-party companies that will put these numbers together for you. The three companies that I recommend are Real Market Reports,

Broker Metrics, and Altos Reports.

It's important to be educated on the property; if this property is an expired listing, know who it expired with and days it was on the market. You need to know the history. You want to be very educated on the property so there are no surprises at the appointment and so you can be completely prepared with your positioning and presentation.

Have all the listing paperwork filled out and typed up in advance. Expect to take this listing. The last thing you want to do is show up, get the okay for the listing, and have nothing prepared. Go prepared to leave the appointment with the signed listing.

Do all of these things prior to your appointment, and you will dramatically increase your success of conversion, and you will consistently walk away with the listing.

GET YOUR GAME FACE ON

What does it mean to have our game face on? I describe it as a "confident swagger you bring out when you are about to get ready to tackle something difficult, take on a challenge, or get down to hard business."

Before you leave for a listing appointment, part of your preparation should be mental. You have already physically prepared for the presentation, but now it's time to get in the right mindset. Be confident, practice your presentation, and review all potential obstacles in advance to know how to overcome potential objections.

This would be a great time to bring out your alter ego. Do anything and everything that gets you into your 100% confident mode so you go into the meeting acting like the authority. Get your game face on; walk in and execute the four-step process for mastering the listing presentation.

THE FOUR-STEP LISTING PRESENTATION PROCESS

There is a four-step process to use at the actual appointment. The four steps are Rapport, Review, Results, and Reality. I'm going to give you a high level look at each step and then dive deeper into the process.

STEP 1: RAPPORT
1. The walk-up
   - Be prepared before you get out of the car.
   - Think confidence, positivity, and enthusiasm.
   - Begin looking for conversation starters.

2. First contact
   - Open with a solid greeting (i.e., "It is an absolute pleasure to finally meet you").
   - Offer a firm handshake.
   - Look the prospect in the eye.
   - Smile.
   - Get permission before acting (i.e., "May I set my things down at the kitchen table?").

3. Grand tour
   - Ask who wants to give you the grand tour of the home.
     - o Determine which of the prospects is in control.
     - o Take the lead.
     - o Let them know you are in control.
   - Discover their FORD
     - o Family
     - o Occupation
     - o Recreation
     - o Dreams

4. Tips
   - Ask, "May I please have a glass of water?" (This establishes control).
   - Don't be excessively enthusiastic about the home.
   - Create doubt by pointing out things that could use updating.
   - Remember that the grand tour is about creating rapport—keep on track.

Rapport is by far the most important of the four steps. You can mess up all the other steps, but do this one right, and you can still win. Remember the liking principle—people do business with people they like. Put a lot of focus on building rapport as first impressions count. The fact that you have an appointment means you have already begun the rapport process, but it is critical to continue building rapport at the appointment. While establishing a relationship, you have to come across as professional, put out a positive vibe, and let them know with confidence that you are the person of choice to represent them. It's important to master this quickly. And it all begins with the walk-up.

What's the walk-up? It's the point from when you park your car in front of their house and you walk up to their front door. It's important to be prepared at this point. Be prepared before you ever get out of your car. Be confident, be positive, be enthusiastic. Remember, you're expecting to take this listing, and when you get out of the car, start looking for conversation starters. Look at what type of car is in the driveway, or maybe there is a motorcycle. Does it have a bumper sticker on it, and if so, what does it say? Look for any clues that will give insight into their interests. Are there kids' toys in the front yard? What type of flag is flying in the front yard? Are there things you can see in the windows? Look for those conversation starters. Finding conversation starters will help you build immediate rapport.

On the walk-up, I suggest you bring your lockbox. Give the seller the perception that you intend to leave with their business. I used to take the For Sale sign with me and lean it against the entryway of the porch so they would see me coming with the intention of getting this listing. It all starts with the walk-up.

Next comes the first contact! Be sure to meet them with a strong greeting: "It's an absolute pleasure to finally meet you." Give a solid, firm handshake and look them in the eyes. Ask them if you may set your things down at the kitchen table. The best place to do your listing presentation is at the kitchen table, not on the couch.

Once your things are set down, ask them, "Who wants to give me the grand tour?" Look at body language. Who's in control? Who takes the lead? Which one of the couple (if they're married) answers the question and begins the tour? Study them and understand the dynamic between the two. You want to identify the person who is in control as they are most likely the one to make the ultimate decision about the listing. Remember, you are really the one in control.

Now the grand tour begins. The seller is about to take you through the property, and I want you to remember this acronym. This is going to help you build the relationship while you're walking through the property. The acronym is FORD. FORD stands for Family, Occupation, Recreation, and Dreams.

Family. Family is the most important thing in many people's lives, and finding out more about their family is a fast way to build rapport. Comment on their family photos; notice how their family is displayed throughout the home, and where possible, even find commonalities. Be attentive to the makeup of their family life.

Occupation. People like to talk about what they do for a living. It is either their greatest area of pain or their greatest area of joy. Expressing interest in their occupation lets them know you care about them beyond just gaining their business.

Recreation. For some, the reason they "do life" is for their hobbies and recreation. This is what *doing life* means to them—participating in recreational activities that bring out their true passion. Are they a golfer, a fisherman, a photographer? Find out what they're interested in, and be interested along with them.

Dreams. Look for clues about the things they dream about. Does their artwork include sailboats? Maybe they have a vision board that lists out more of their dreams. Ask about their future and the next steps in their lives and learn about their dreams. Get them thinking about their future.

While you're on the walk-through, transition so you take the lead. Be intentional and ask questions that build rapport using the FORD concept. And as you walk around, be careful not to be too enthusiastic about the property. Don't say too much about the property itself; too much praise or enthusiasm can create an elevated opinion of the property's worth on behalf of the seller. Don't beat the property down; just don't say too much about it in general. Focus on FORD because you're going to point out the flaws and create some doubt, and building rapport is important for them to be able to handle that.

STEP 2: REVIEW

1. Set the seller's expectations of this appointment.
   - Review
   - Marketing
   - Market

2. Tell them that after this appointment, one of three things is going to happen:
   - You have the opportunity to list your home with me.
   - You decide not to list with me.
   - I decide it's not a fit and choose to not take your listing.

3. Share with them that after the appointment, regardless of the outcome, they will be more educated on the process of what needs to happen to successfully sell the property.

4. Ask them if they have any questions before you begin.

5. Review the Seller Discovery Sheet with them.
   - Recap the previous conversations and what you already know to clarify their needs and motivation.
   - Confirm why they are selling.
   - Ask if they have sold a home before.
   - Inquire as to whether they are also buying a new home.
   - Question whether they have an idea of what their home will sell for.

6. Find their pain.
   - Dig deep.
   - Ask the hard questions.
   - Paint the picture for them in great detail.

Remember, after the tour, when you're at the kitchen table, ask for a glass of water. This is a great way to take control, and we want the seller to perceive us as the person that's in control. As part of the review process, your goal is to find their true motivation for selling. You are also going to set the seller's expectation of this appointment. Let the seller know you want to go through the Seller Discovery Sheet and review their situation.

Once you have clarity, let them know you want to share with them marketing of the property and why you sell homes faster than the average agent in the area. From there, let them know you will discuss today's market. Then you will get into the numbers, showing them what the market is like today, the average number of days on the market, what the property needs to be priced at, and what sales have been for comparable properties. Once you set their expectations, ask them if they have any questions before you begin. You have now established control and authority over the appointment.

When delivering the next piece of the presentation, I recommend you use one of two tactics. They are similar and either way works. It utilizes the scarcity principle to further draw the seller into choosing you. The first tactic would be to let the seller know that after this appointment, there will be one of three outcomes:

1. You decide to list your home with me.

2. You decide not to list your home with me.

3. I decide it's not a fit and choose not to take the listing.

The second tactic would be to tell the seller this: "After this appointment, there's a good chance that we may or may not do business together, because I do turn down more listings than I take. I promise you this, though: after the end of this appointment, you're going to be more educated on the process so you can make a more logical decision on where you want to go from here. The last thing you want is your listing expiring or not selling for top dollar, right?" They respond affirmatively, which gives you the opportunity to add, "So you understand the importance of hiring the right real estate agent this time around." You've now established authority and scarcity.

Now you can go ahead and begin the review process. You begin with the Seller's Discovery Sheet so you can recap the previous conversations. The Seller's Discovery Sheet will clarify their motivation. You want to know things like why they're selling, whether they have ever sold a home before, if they are buying a home, and if they have an idea of what their property is going to sell for. Every seller has a number in their head of what their property's worth, and it's important that we get that to see how realistic they are in understanding their home's value.

Another reason for reviewing the Seller's Discovery Sheet is that you want to uncover their pain. If you don't find their pain, you don't stand a chance. It's simply taking the conversations you've already had with them and doing a review. You want to do this by digging deep - asking the hard questions based on their motivations. If someone wants to be in their new location by a certain date, ask them what happens if they aren't there by then. This will paint the picture for them about not achieving their goal. Their answer will also tell you how important that motivation really is to them. Review everything you know from your discovery, and clarify their motivation or pain. This will help you know how to proceed with the results.

STEP 3: RESULTS

1. Introduce your team and their roles.
   - You/Listing Specialist
   - Assistant
   - Listing Coordinator
   - Transaction Coordinator
   - Buyer's Agents
   - Inside Sales Associates
   - Vendors/Partners

2. Provide proof through statistics and facts.
   - Homes listed vs. homes sold
   - List to sales price ratio
   - Number of homes sold

3. Share five things you do differently.

- Back page of *Homes and Land* magazine
- 800 call capture/auto text message info
- Aggressive online presence
- Outbound telemarketing team
- Network of agents and investors
- Specialized marketing programs
- Social media marketing
- Relocation services
- Open House system

4. Offer your marketing arsenal guarantees (as fits their pain).
   - Performance Guarantee
   - Smart Seller Program
   - Easy Exit Listing
   - Communication Guarantee
   - Marketing Plan
   - Other specialized programs

Results for the seller is about marketing. Based on what you know about them and why they're selling and what is most important to them, you are going to talk to them about what you do differently to market their property to get it sold. You will customize your presentation according to what you have discovered. If a performance guarantee isn't important and its never been mentioned it previously, then don't make that offer. If the appointment is for an expired listing, there is no need to discuss the Smart Seller Program, because we already know they have listed it and do not want to sell on their own

It's very important that the seller sees you as an agent that can successfully sell their property. Give them a sense that you only take listings that you believe you can sell. They have to sense that. In addition to the CMA, you need to use third party reports with all the charts, graphs, statistics. You've got to know exactly what makes these people tick. Do you need to talk about the communication guarantee? Do you talk about making it risk-free in the Easy Exit Listing? Do you talk about your Smart Seller Program?

At this point in the appointment, introduce your team and each of their roles in helping to get your seller's home sold. Explain that you are the listing agent and you have a team working in various parallel roles to market and sell their property. If you don't have a full team behind you at this point, use those around you that assist in the process. Everybody has a team. The receptionist at your real estate office is a team member, and think outside the box for the remaining team members. Use your lender, your coach, and your mentor. Give the seller the perception that you have a team of people surrounding you because of your success. Tell them about your vendors and your preferred partners. Create a one sheet that introduces your entire team. Helping them see that you have a team surrounding you gives them confidence in your ability to sell their home.

Part of what establishes you as an authority is to share with them statistics and facts. There are three statistics that are important to be able to share with the seller about you. The first one is homes listed vs. homes sold. Compare it to the overall MLS (Multiple Listing Service) statistic. For example, share with your seller that 20% of all homes listed fail to sell. That's one in five homes. Contrast that with the fact that you sell 90% of your homes listed because of your team, your customized marketing, and because you specialize in listing and selling homes. If you are a new agent and don't have your own statistics, use the statistics of your agency or your broker.

The second statistic you want to share is your list price to sales price ratio, and how well that performs for the averages in your market. Share the price difference they can expect to make by listing with you because of your marketing efforts focused on getting the maximum amount and selling it in the fastest amount of time.

The third statistic to share is your homes sold vs. the MLS average. For example, your team sold more than 157 homes when the average agent only sells 4 homes a year. It's important to hit on that statistic. Tell them that the average agent only sells four homes a year, and even if you only sell 25 homes, that's still a much greater percentage. Know these numbers and leverage them to attain the listing.

Once you have established rapport and reviewed your findings to find their pain and have shared statistics with the seller, pick five things that you do differently than everybody else. Perhaps you do ads on the back page of *Homes and Land* magazine, you have a great online presence, you utilize social media marketing, or you offer drone aerial photography. Choose five things that you will do that differentiate you from your competitors. Let them know how you plan to get results for them.

Share with the seller your Marketing Arsenal and how you will use the appropriate guarantees to sell their home twice as fast as another agent. Find the guarantee that fits their motivation (pain) and add it to your plan to give the seller additional confidence that you are the right agent for their listing.

STEP 4: REALITY
1. Pound the pain.
   - Use statistics, graphs, and charts.
   - There is proof in numbers.
   - Buyers determine the real estate pricing market.

2. Utilize Market Trend Reports.
   - Create more pain.
   - Be ultra-confident in your ability to read and present the information.

3. Solve their problem.

4. Motivate action by emotional factors.
   - Fear
   - Guilt
   - Love
   - Pride

5. Complete the Home Selling Process.
   - Set seller's expectations.
   - Communicate.
   - Generate next steps.
   - Give homework to seller.
   - Set the listing term.
   - Set up a home staging consultation.

• Put a "Coming Soon" sign in yard.

The last step in the four-step process is reality. This is where you talk with the seller about pricing. Be sure to take the report that you had prepared from your third party source. When you use third party reports, you have impartial statistics to back up your pricing strategy.

To segue into the reality step, ask the seller whether they will allow you to list the property at a price that will allow your marketing to work. You've already shared the statistics of your marketing, and it works. Then show them the numbers. Your goal is simple. It's to get them to be realistic, and to get them to be realistic you need to use everything you possibly can to get them to understand what a realistic price is for listing their home.

Here is an important point: The sellers do not determine what their home is worth. Their payoff doesn't determine what their home is worth. Who does? The buyers, a.k.a., the marketplace. You don't want to take this listing if the seller is not going to be realistic. If they aren't realistic, you will be wasting your time and money on the listing. Being direct is important. If you're a softy and you're not direct, then it's hard to get them to listen to your expertise. Stand your ground as the authority, and get the prospect to price their home at a realistic price.

Share the market trends report. I highly recommend utilizing these reports as they will pay for themselves just by sharing the visual graphs and charts. In today's market, more people are being unrealistic, but the reason they're being unrealistic is because nobody's given them the perspective they need. That's what these reports do.

Reiterate the information you've gathered. Utilize emotional factors to get them to make a decision. People act on emotion, and the biggest motivators are fear, guilt, love, and pride. Use emotional triggers to get them to make a decision.

Once you have shared the information, ask the seller this question: "Based on the information that you've just seen, at what price would you like to put your property on the market today?" Then shut up. If they give you a number that is realistic based on the information you presented, ask them, "Are there any questions before we begin the paperwork?"

You already have the paperwork mostly filled out, and you just have to fill in the blanks. Remember that the seller has a goal. You're sitting there in the appointment for a reason. Why are they meeting with a real estate agent? Why did they agree to meet with you and talk to you about putting their home on the market? They want to sell their home. Find out what their motivation is, provide the solution, get them to be realistic on their sales price, and capture the listing.

Now that you have secured the listing, you need to give the seller their homework. Give them a seller's disclosure notice to complete. Talk to the seller about the home staging consultation that you are going set up and explain its importance, because it's a fact that a staged home sells faster than a property that's not staged; it also sells for more money. Tell them you're going set up a home staging consultation with a third-party home stager that you have a relationship with, and the consultation is going to be totally free. Talk to them about why decluttering the home and removing items that make it too personal helps the buyers be able to imagine themselves in the home. Walk back through the home with the seller giving them a buyer's perspective.

REPETITION BREEDS MASTERY. AND MASTERY LEADS TO GREATLY IMPROVED SUCCESS.

Don't be in a hurry to just throw the home on the market. This is important. Be in a hurry to get them to sign the listing, but not to put the property on the market, because you want the property to be staged before a buyer ever shows up. Have them be a part of this process. You can even put your For Sale sign in the front yard with a Coming Soon sign rider. This is a great way to generate interest in the home before it goes active.

REPETITION LEADS TO MASTERY

The listing presentation doesn't need to be longer than 50 minutes. If you are going on appointments longer than 50 minutes, you're talking too much. Keep that in mind. Follow the process, and always do the same thing. Stick to the process and master it.

Focus on delivering more value and becoming more confident, but the actual presentation needs to be a true system. Repetition breeds mastery. And mastery leads to greatly improved success.

ACTIONS TO TAKE

1. Practice using FORD to build rapport (Family, Occupation, Recreation, Dreams).
2. Create a presentation outline based on the four-step process.
3. Have a comprehensive Seller Discovery Sheet completed prior to the appointment.
4. Find a good marketing report service if you don't already have one.

KEYS TO SUCCESS

1. Rapport trumps everything.
2. One of the biggest mistakes that you can ever make is going on appointments that aren't qualified.
3. Go prepared *and expecting* to leave the appointment with the signed listing.
4. Before you leave for a listing appointment, part of your preparation should be mental.
5. To master your listing presentations, utilize the four-step process: Rapport, Review, Results, and Reality.
6. Repetition breeds mastery, and mastery leads to greatly improved success.

9. Get Buyers to Take Action

*The aim of marketing is to know and understand
the customer so well the service fits him and sells itself.*
—Peter Drucker

S o many real estate agents today are spending too much effort generating buyer leads and not maximizing their opportunities with the leads they have already generated. You're investing a significant amount of money in online buyer lead generation systems. You have a website that's generating traffic, you get calls from yard signs where people are wanting to know the price of a home, and you have referrals coming in the door. Those are great things, because you need to have leads. It is not enough to get the leads, though, if you don't convert those leads into money.

What you really need is to lock down the formula that gets buyers to take the most action. That's when you begin to get conversions. You need to do things that will have buyers perceiving you as the trusted authority. Then you will be the undisputed expert in your field.

HOW TO BE A REAL ESTATE EXPERT

In the new era, how you communicate with your buyers, and how you present and position your services, is going to make you stand apart from all other agents. The new-era buyer, right now, already knows all of the different properties that they want to see (or they think that they do because of all the resources online), and they don't think they have as much of a need for the real estate agent as they once did.

You're selling to the buyer who thinks they don't need an agent, who thinks they can go out there and do it all on their own, and who thinks that they can wait until kingdom come to go out there and purchase the home. To get the buyer to treat you like you are the expert and not them, you have to BE the expert. And to be the expert, you need to (1) educate and inform, (2) take the buyer offline, (3) set expectations, and (4) create a sense of urgency.

1. EDUCATE AND INFORM

With every single buyer lead that you generate, I want you to do two things. The first is to have a go-to positioning offer, something of value that you can give away. It can be a book, a free report, a free offer of your services, or a free strategy session. Think about what it is that the buyer wants that you can give them immediately without expecting anything in return and give it to them. It doesn't have to cost anything, but it has to be something of value. Giving them something of value makes them believe that you care about them and not just you. It also makes them see that you go beyond the norm and sets you up as an authority when you are presenting them with unexpected value.

Have these value pieces readily available as part of your marketing arsenal. You need to be prepared for all the possible scenarios of your buyer's pain and perceived need, and respond immediately with something of value to them that shows that you listened and heard their desires and that you can get them what they asked for as well— confirm to them you can solve their problem. Do it immediately.

The second thing I want you to do is shoot a video with your mobile phone and send your buyer lead a personalized video within the first five minutes of making contact. This is as simple as sending a text message with today's mobile technology, but your buyer will perceive it is something very unique and personal just for them.

What's a video message going to do? It will cut through the clutter. Information is abundant. The amount of information we see in one day is the amount of information our ancestors would receive in 50 years!

I'm not playing around with this rule. It is going to set you apart. Your top priority is to make it personal. Otherwise, you might as well stop investing in buyer leads and throwing your money away. If you fail to send them a personalized video message within the first five minutes, you are going to try to fix their problem in other ways, and doing this one thing is going to get you different results. So, shoot them a video and stop making excuses. I don't care how you look or if you're nervous; you're good enough to shoot a 30-second video and let your buyer see you. Inject enthusiasm into your video, and people will love you.

What does your video message sound like? I'm going to give you a couple of examples, and then you can tailor them to your situation. You will get it after you do a few, but until then, follow a script if you need to, but remove whatever excuse you have for just not getting it done.

Here we go …

Hit record and say something like this:

"Hey, Shirley, thank you so much for going to MyHousePage. com and filling out the form for more information. I hope that you found the properties that you're looking for; at least you got a good start. What I'm going to do is this: I'm going to send you a quick list of the Top 10 Best Deals in your area, because as you know, we're one of the top teams in the area. A lot of buyers love how we're able to find properties that are not on the MLS. I want to show you an example of that, so check your email and grab that list. Again, I just want to put a face to the name: I'm Hoss Pratt. I'm here to serve you, I'm here to help you, and I'm looking forward to connecting with you. So go ahead and check your email, and if you have any questions, you let me know, Shirley. Thank you so much, and I'll talk to you soon!"

Here's another example …

"Hey, Steve! Thanks for filling out the form on my website for more information. I'm here to help; I'm here to serve. I want you to know that I just sent you some information directly to your email. It's a free ebook, Moving Forward: 25 Essential Rules to Know When Buying or Selling a Home. *Take a glance and read through the book. I particularly love chapter 19, and I think you will too! If you have any questions, let me know, and I'll be in touch."*

It's that simple. Keep the momentum going. Don't overthink it, just do it. Make it quick and easy and personal. Create and send the video immediately within the first five minutes of getting the lead to show the buyer they're important to you.

Connect with the buyer, and give them an offer of value up front. Remember, your buyer leads are going to your competitor's websites as well. They didn't just seek you out. They are more focused on properties, so you need to give them a reason to choose you. At this point, they have no loyalty. Don't lose a buyer because you failed to act. Make the commitment now to get buyers off the fence. Reach them personally within the first five minutes. It's the #1 rule of buyer conversion in the new era.

> DON'T LOSE A BUYER BECAUSE YOU FAILED TO ACT.

2. TAKE THE BUYER OFFLINE

How do you get your buyers offline? You either need to set an appointment or get them on the phone. You've got to start a conversation. That's why the video's so important. It's easier to get them offline when they already feel that connection with you.

Offline is where the rubber meets the road. This is where the relationship is established. In today's busy world, buyers have so many options. Online, there's so much noise. Buyers are on Facebook, Twitter, Instagram, Pinterest, online shopping, email, and everywhere.

Imagine this, a buyer is looking for a home. They go to Zillow, and Zillow has retargeting. So now they see Zillow everywhere in their newsfeeds. They visit a website: "Mike Smith, Realtor Extraordinaire." Mike's a smart guy, he has Facebook retargeting, and now that buyer is seeing Zillow and Mike everywhere. Are they seeing you? That's the noise you're competing against. You have to get them out of the noise by taking them offline. Then you can get their undivided attention and establish a relationship.

Reach the buyer, get them offline, and deliver personalized content, which helps you with expert positioning. It is important for you to create more content and educational material that is specific to your local marketplace. Bring in the people that know the content better than you, like your local community leaders, and use them as added value in unique ways the buyers won't expect to promote the benefits of the local market in which they are looking to buy. Reach out to your local mayors, the school board president, and those people that will be able to provide a level of experience for your buyers where they'll be able to learn more about your local marketplace than anywhere else. That's how you crush Zillow. Zillow will never be able to create localized, personalized content like I'm telling you to do. And most of your competitors will let the Internet do their work for them. Set yourself apart.

In the new era, the buyer wants to work with the expert. You're the expert. Are you delivering localized, personalized content? It's up to you to educate your buyer. Don't rely on drip campaigns alone. That's a thing of the past!

If you've been in the real estate business for any length of time, you know all the CRM options in the business. You are aware of other marketing systems that help you connect with your leads automatically. It's hard to automate the personalization. I'm not telling you to stop doing any automation, but the buyer needs to believe you have a personal connection with them, so be sure to include personal touches along with your other efforts if you want to be seen as different and get them out of the noise of everything else.

Everybody is going to feel warmth, loved on, and like they are cared for because you're not one of those agents out there who is trying to avoid the personalization because that is easiest for you. You make it about them, and that is when you earn their trust. Instead, get comfortable with being uncomfortable and deliver localized, personalized educational content to give your buyers a reason to choose you over your competition.

Start creating educational materials on your local marketplace and start educating your buyers. Be their expert. That's the value of the future of real estate agents. If you start leveraging more of this in your business, you'll not only generate more buyer leads, but you'll get **GET COMFORTABLE WITH BEING UNCOMFORTABLE.** more buyers to jump off the fence and say, "Yes!" Set yourself apart, or you may find yourself obsolete. Someone will do the work. It might as well be you. You don't have to do hard things to set yourself apart, but you have to do things. Being the same as everybody else isn't going to cut it in this era.

I believe that becoming the expert is paramount to your success. Get to know your community leaders and experts and become *the most resourceful agent for your market*. Leverage technology and build a marketing arsenal, and you'll be ahead of the curve. Follow these steps, take massive determined action, and you will have buyers hopping off the fence in droves.

3. SET EXPECTATIONS

Imagine you've done everything right so far: you've educated and informed the buyer, they've come to your office, you're meeting with them, they love you, and you're sitting down with them. Now is when you're really going to establish your value. You need to make them understand you expect to get their business. Your expectations will include statements like these:

- This is why I get paid what I get paid.
- This is why I do what I do.
- This is how I'm going to be able to help you find properties out there that are going to be a perfect fit, get you your dream home, and save you as much money as possible.
- This is why I'm the best at what I do.
- This is why I get more repeat referral business than any other agent out there.

This is a process that most agents don't have, and if they had it, it would solve a lot of their problems.

If you have a team, you have buyer agents that you're working with, and you have a process like this, it's easier for the baton to get passed; it's easier for the hand-off. Make sure the expectations are set.

I want you to think about your marketing arsenal. This should be a way to separate you from everybody else, to have a program that people instantly see value in. This has everything to do with setting expectations and branding. You want everything that you do to be branded, to be coveted, and to leave your prospects thinking, "What else is there?" This is where you establish your value.

4. CREATE A SENSE OF URGENCY

When working with buyers, it is important to create a sense of urgency. While you don't want to pressure someone into making a decision that is not right for them, oftentimes buyers will sit on the fence so long that the home they decide to make an offer on has already been sold, and then the process has to start over from square one.

Jim Rohn says, "Without a sense of urgency, desire loses its value." To me, that's a brilliant statement. How do you create a sense of urgency with your buyers? There are multiple ways.

One way to create a sense of urgency is to use the Scarcity Principle. By letting the buyer know that the home will not be on the market long because it is priced competitively, it is in a hot market, or that a lot of interest has been shown with multiple offers expected can all be ways of letting the buyer know that they could lose out on the property if they don't act quickly.

Another reason to act quickly in today's market is that there are indicators pointing to interest rates going up. In order to lock in current rates, it is important to act now. This can end up costing them tens of thousands of dollars over the course of the mortgage loan. Appeal to this pain of costing more money to create a sense of urgency.

You can also use current events or situations to create a sense of urgency. Things happening in the stock market is an example; an election year creates uncertainty and volatility is another example. Create an element of fear of the unknown by waiting due to current conditions. Be sure to help remove the buyer's reluctance by creating a sense of urgency. Close the deal and get your buyer in their new home!

> WITHOUT A SENSE OF URGENCY, DESIRE LOSES ITS VALUE.
>
> –JIM ROHN

Most of all, remember to do those things with your buyer that will set you up in their mind as an undisputed authority and expert. Make it so the buyer feels like they would be making the wrong decision not to choose you. Make it easy for them to choose you, and then over deliver.

THE FIVE-STEP HOME
BUYING PROCESS

On the phone you want to prepare the buyer for the five-step home buying process that you will present during the appointment. It will show that you have a system for what you're doing and that utilizing that system will save them money. Below is an example of a conversation to have to set up the appointment. Use this script or modify it to fit your specific situation.

What I want you to do, Mr. Buyer, is come in Thursday at seven o'clock. I'm going to show you my five-step home buying process, which is the reason that we're a repeat referral business, more so than any other agent in the market. My five-step home buying process is responsible for not only saving tens of thousands of dollars and hundreds of hours of time, but it is able to find the homes in the market that perfectly fit your needs. My team and I are the best at this.

The reason I am the best is because I have this five-step home buying process that is going to take you step by step (from point A to Z) through everything that you need to be able to find your dream home. That's where we're going to start, Thursday at seven o'clock, when you come to the office, does that time work for you?

Using this script will allow you to use the five-step process to establish the value on the phone when they're offline. You leave them thinking, "What does he know that I don't know?" What you want is for them to want to know more. Make the Five-Step Home Buying Process YOUR Five-Step Home Buying Process. Own this, brand this. Your value as an agent depends on you giving them this process. Here are the five steps.

STEP 1: NEEDS ANALYSIS

The Needs Analysis step is an in-depth way to understand your buyer's needs with crystal clarity. Through a series of questions, you will determine exactly the type of property the buyer is looking to purchase:

- What kind of home are you looking for: condo, house, town-home?

- What area of town? Which neighborhood? Why?

- What's your price point?

- What size OR square footage are you looking for?

STEP 2: HOME SELECTION

In the Home Selection step, establish your authority, provide value, and shine! Go to work. Show them what the competitors can't do. You want your buyers to be blown away when they see the type of value that a real expert brings to the transaction. The Home Selection step helps buyers realize that they don't have all of the power that you do, that they just can't just download an app and find every property that's available on the market. This step establishes you as the expert and the saving grace in finding their dream home. Don't just look at properties on the MLS. Utilize your network: agents, strategic partners, builders, and investors. You're going to look under every rock and stone, sideways and upside-down, for the home that was identified in the Needs Analysis step.

STEP 3: HOME PREVIEW

When it comes to the Home Preview step, narrow down the selection to 5–15 homes that perfectly match your buyer's criteria. You're not going to look at 30 homes. You've already set expectations. You don't need to look at 30 homes. You don't need to waste time when you set expectations up front. This step is where your buyer agent comes in. This is typically when the handoff is made. Note, you will look for things like: How does it feel? How does the energy of the home feel? The neighborhood? What do you first see? What is the feeling? What's around you? What's your first impression? All of these are important in the Home Preview.

STEP 4: CRAFTING THE OFFER

When you craft the offer, make the magic happen! This is your secret sauce, something that's really important and when things get serious. You're going to sit down with the buyer, review the dream homes identified, and pick one to craft an offer. You've got to put passion and energy behind this, because that's where you establish your value.

Talking with Your Buyer about the Offer

You found a perfect home! It's your dream home. You never thought you could ever find a home as perfect as this one, but you found it. Now imagine that you were writing an offer for this home and you weren't working with an expert, like us. Imagine the seller in this process. They may have a stack of offers like this (show them a stack of folders to help them visualize).

Here we have eight different offers on this property, eight people who think that this home is their dream home. How does your offer stick out? By crafting the perfect offer. Imagine losing this dream home right now because someone else crafted a better offer than us. This is something that's so important to me because I don't want any of my buyers to ever lose a dream home. I take it so seriously. That's why I created the perfect formula to craft the perfect offer: I want, out of every single one of these offers, for ours to jump up to the front of the line, to stand out as a no-brainer. And it's not just about pricing.

There are seven different parts of the contract that I go through. I know how to give them an offer that they can't refuse. This is how I earn my keep. This is why I do what I do. Are you ready to craft the perfect offer? Let's go get your dream home. Let's go make this thing happen!

Own this step of the process. Do exactly what I'm saying and add enthusiasm to your process, because this is the value of the real estate agent in the new era. The marketplace wants the agent that fixes the problem, that delivers what they want, and makes it happen. So step it up!

STEP 5: CONTRACT TO CLOSE

In the Contract to Close step, you provide your buyer with certainty with your experience and expertise. Be prepared! At this point the inspection is happening, and the inspector is going to send a pages-long inspection report over that's going to terrify your buyer. They're going to think, "What happened to my dream home? What's wrong with my dream home?" And you're going to tell them nothing's wrong with their dream home in most cases. Tell them that inspectors get paid to find every little thing. Remind them to trust you during this process and set their expectations accordingly:

> *This is why we created the perfect formula to close. This is how we ensure that you will get your keys on closing day. We've all heard the horror story: the person who packed up and sold everything, just to see the closing fall apart at the last minute. That's not what you get with us. You get certainty. You get professionalism. You get experience. You get expertise. You get a make-it-happen attitude. That's what you get when you work with us.*

ACTIONS TO TAKE

1. Create your customized video script template and record a practice video. Practice, and then execute with an actual prospect.
2. Deliver localized, personalized educational content to give your buyers a reason to choose you over your competition.

KEYS TO SUCCESS

1. What you really need is to lock down the formula that gets buyers to take the most action. Then you will be the undisputed expert in your field.
2. The new-era buyer, right now, already knows all of the different properties that they want to see (or they think they do because of all the resources online), and they don't think they have as much of a need for the real estate agent as they once did. You have to make them see you as the expert.
3. Don't lose a buyer because you failed to act.

4. Get comfortable with being uncomfortable.

5. Without a sense of urgency, desire loses its value.

6. Join **Listing Boss Academy**. See my invitation on page 201

10. Build a Winning Team

Talent wins games, but teamwork and intelligence wins championships.
—MICHAEL JORDAN

If you're just starting out in the business, you may be thinking this chapter isn't for you. I want you to absorb everything I'm going to share with you here, however, because this will be about your future growth and freedom. You will be able to visualize what you need to do in order to build a winning, high-performing team that will dramatically increase your earning potential.

It isn't enough to build a team; you need to build the right team to get the results you really want. Each of those team members needs to support your values, fill your gaps, and deliver results in their specific roles. How do you build a winning team?

BUILD YOURSELF FIRST

Are you currently maximizing yourself? This is something that's very important because remember, the number one term in business is allocation: allocation of your time, your money, and your resources. Are you currently getting the most out of you? Are you being the best you, you can be? Are you managing your day to the best of your potential? Are you focused on money-making activities? It's really going to be hard to lead from the front if you aren't doing these things, and that's what I want to share with you—leading from the front.

The reason you have the need to build a team is because your time is already being maximized, and you need more resources to help you deliver and grow. This chapter is not about what you need when you are first getting into the business. This chapter is about growth and building to achieve your vision and goals. You need other talent to pick up the tasks that are holding you back. The way to grow is to delegate to a team who specialize in specific areas of the business.

I want you to put on your reading list a book by Michael Gerber called *The E-Myth*. I encourage you to read it because this book will change your paradigm forever. In the book Gerber talks about how to build a business and how there are so many different personalities. We try to be the manager, the entrepreneur, or the technician—the one cure-all, end-all person that's going to do everything. The problem is that you really can't. You have your strengths and weaknesses, and you have your capacity. What you need to do is maximize your strengths and delegate your weaknesses.

Your goal is to work on your business, not in your business. That's your ultimate goal; that's freedom.

There are six key hires (excluding you) that will help you build a winning team. You are a big role in this whole team concept. You are the leader. Your job as the leader is to focus on lead generation and strategizing. Your job is also to hire, fire, and manage. Hire slow, fire fast, manage, inspire, and lead. It is your responsibility to train, coach, and consult to make your team become more valuable, because the more valuable your team becomes, the more value you deliver to the marketplace and the more money you're going to make. You've got to meet with your staff members, hold them accountable to their goals, and strategize for them.

> **FREEDOM IS BEING ABLE TO WORK ON YOUR BUSINESS AND NOT HAVE TO WORK IN YOUR BUSINESS.**

LEAD FROM THE FRONT

The most important thing is, it doesn't matter how big of a team you build, but it's very important to lead from the front. Here's what I mean by that. You want to set the standard and live the standard. Just because you have a team doesn't mean that you stop lead generating. For example, you lead generate more than ever because your team is going to see you, and it's going to rub off on them that they better pick up the phone and prospect because that is the standard with your team.

Success also attracts talent. You can't avoid this. People are going to come find you if you are successful, and they will want to be a part of your team because they see the success. You want a team that is unshakeable and that shares your vision and purpose. Make sure your team clearly understands your vision and that your goal as a team is to be the best that you can be. Your team will look to you to be their leader, and they will look to see what you *do*. Winners lead from the front. Successful people share their purpose with their team and live that purpose daily in such a way that it becomes contagious. Work on yourself first so you can be the leader that others want to follow. Make sure your vision is clear and that you set your team up to win.

KEY HIRES

There are six key hires to make in building a winning team. They are

Transaction Coordinator	Inside Sales Associate (ISA)
Administrative Assistant	Listing Coordinator
Buyer/Showing Agent	Listing Agent

Right now, you could be filling all of those roles. Once your business grows, you can't be everything to everybody in every role. You have to delegate and maximize your strengths and fill your weaknesses. Remember the chart back under time management that showed how much your time was worth? It isn't a good return on investment for you to be spending your time doing assistant tasks and filling roles that keep you from staying focused on generating revenue.

Transaction Coordinator. I believe the first key hire should be the transaction coordinator. The transaction coordinator's job on your team is to handle the contract to the close. As soon as you execute a contract, that customer is transitioned to the transaction coordinator whose job it is to ensure that that property closes successfully. That's it. That's the sole job of the transaction coordinator. They manage all the lenders, the home inspectors, the appraisers, the title company, the other agent, and anything else the customer needs until they close. At first, it may be difficult to delegate. It is hard to believe that someone else can handle the details like you can. It is important, however, to stay out of the way and let them do their job so you can stay focused on yours. There is only so much of you to go around, and the best use of your time is to stay leveraged on those activities that increase your revenue. Take the time to hire the right people, and then believe in them and their ability to get the job done.

The transaction coordinator is a very important hire, because the tasks involved can monopolize a lot of your time. Create a system that is easy to follow, and hire someone committed to the process. It is also someone you can add to your team without upfront overhead. Most transaction coordinators will earn anywhere between $250-$350 per transaction, paid at closing. It can be a flat fee role that more than pays for itself by the time you get to the first closing simply by the time you've put back into your own schedule. A good place to begin looking for a transaction coordinator is at other brokerages. You can also find virtual assistants through many online sources who are more than capable of fulfilling the role of the transaction coordinator. There may even be other agents in your office that could use the guaranteed money and who would be interested in taking on this role. They are already used to only getting paid at closing, so a flat fee could be attractive to them.

The transition coordinator will fulfill a role that has to be executed and that can take up a disproportionate amount of your time. Get those tasks off your plate in a way that has no risk associated to you— you are only paying on contracts that end up closing, so there are no hidden costs. Think about what you can accomplish in the time saved from one closing transaction. For example, let's just say you would have spent 10 hours fulfilling all the tasks of a transaction coordinator. In the same time frame, if you spent that time prospecting and got one listing or found a home for one buyer, you will have spent $250-$350 and made thousands. If you are spending your own time being the transaction coordinator, that opportunity for revenue is lost and cannot be recouped. You are losing money by being your own transaction coordinator.

I understand that until you reach a certain number, you count on the revenue, and you need to fulfill more roles. A good rule of thumb is to bring on your transaction coordinator and an assistant when you get to that $5- to $10-million mark in production. That is typically representative of things getting busier than you can handle because

IT'S NEVER TOO EARLY TO BRING ON THE TRANSACTION COORDINATOR, BECAUSE YOU DON'T HAVE TO PAY THEM UNTIL THE DEAL CLOSES. of the volume that you're doing. This is not a perfect science, but is a good rule of thumb.

When you get to $10 million in production, you will want to bring on a buyer's agent and potentially an Inside Sales Associate (ISA). These are tar- gets that I want you to set your sights on achieving. At the $20-million mark in production, you will add on another listing agent. At the $30-million mark, you will want to bring on more of every role.

Remember, it's never too early to bring on the transaction coordinator, because you don't have to pay them until the deal closes. Bring them on as soon as you can possibly afford it, and if you think you can't afford it, test it and see what you are able to do in the time you gain by not having to take care of all those transaction tasks that are must dos.

Administrative Assistant. I want to talk with you about the importance of hiring the administrative assistant when you hit approximately the $4 to $6 million in production mark. They will be your go-to person. The assistant's role will be to prepare for all the lead generation and the system's execution. In the morning they will be the one to send out all your letters. They will be the one who imports the leads into your CRM software. They will be the one to communicate with your sellers. In addition, they will manage other office tasks like office supplies, being a liaison with vendors, and handling your bookkeeping. Paying bills and managing financials is not something that generates revenue for you, and you need to make sure you hire an assistant who understands bookkeeping-someone who can manage this for you or delegate bookkeeping to a professional. Your assistant is a good person to oversee and communicate with your transaction coordinator. They are your eyes and ears for everything.

When hiring your assistant, be sure to look for someone who can take charge and make things happen without taking too much of your time. You will always be the leader of the team, but if you spend too much time managing, you will not get the full benefit of having team members in the first place. Be sure to hire someone you can trust and who can be self-directed to execute on your behalf. Depending on your situation, you may want to initially hire someone part-time who has the ability to grow as the position grows. You have options. The key thing is to make smart decisions with your time and find ways to spend your time on $250/hour activities, and let an administrative assistant handle all the $15-$30/hour tasks.

A good administrative assistant will cost you between $15-$30 an hour. The highest end of this pay scale would be for a great, experienced talent, and it is possible you will only need someone part-time to start. You are literally one hire away from becoming as successful as you want to be. One hire will take your business to the next level. Why? If you can gain back even 10-20 hours per week that you are currently spending doing $20 activities and leverage that time for lead generation, how do you think that's going to turn out for you? You might even want to hire someone on the lower end of the scale around $15 an hour and pay a bonus of $100 for every closing transaction. That way, you have more control over your expenses even though you might end up paying more out in the long run. Find a way to make it work. You can find administrative assistants from most of the same sources as the transaction coordinator … at other agencies, virtual assistant companies, online job sites, real estate schools, and even at the local colleges.

Buyer's Agent. The next key hire I want to discuss is your buyer's agent. You want to consider bringing in a buyer's agent when your production is around the $5- to $10-million mark. In bringing on a buyer's agent, I want you to know this: a lot of how you build your team is going to rely on what you do and what you like to do. For example, in my own business, I didn't want to do anything but go on listing appointments. I wanted to go Monday through Friday and focus on listing appointments, all day every day. I built my business around that. If you want to do nothing but show buyers homes every day, you could build a business around that as well.

The role of the buyer's agent is to secure appointments with buyers and get buyer's agreements signed. Their job is simply to show listings, negotiate offers, and sell homes. They should be on appointments all day every day. You're leading from the front, and they're following your command. You should schedule a weekly meeting with them to motivate them, teach them scripts, and make sure they are using the right systems that will set them up for success.

Now let's get your thinking more outside the box. I believe you should consider bringing on three buyer's agents at one time, for two reasons. One reason is that you want a competitive atmosphere. One of the best ways to get the best out of people is to make them compete. In my own business, I had a white board where I had the agents' results...and everybody could see each other's numbers. I don't know about you, but every time I'm on a board competing with other people, I'm going to be at the top of that board come hell or high water. Salespeople want to compete and win; it drives us and motivates us. The second reason for hiring three agents at one time is simply because you can triple your training efforts by training three at one time instead of a single agent. It maximizes your own efforts.

There are a couple of different options as to how you can pay a buyer's agent. A lot of times, people bring on buyer's agents and pay them straight commission—usually offering them somewhere between a 40%-55% commission from each transaction. You are providing the leads and the marketing. You are training them and giving them the resources they need. They are showing listings, negotiating the deals, and closing the sales.

Another angle to use with the buyer's agent is to consider hiring a showing agent. If you're doing a good job qualifying the appointments, you can set up a showing agent who you pay $10-$15 an hour to simply go show the homes. Your buyer's agent would get the buyer agreement signed, secure the appointment, and negotiate the offers. All you're doing is paying a showing agent to show the listings. It's a more profitable model if you have the volume, but it will also cost you money whether or not listings are closed. If you don't have the volume, it's not as profitable. It's going to cost you more money out of pocket. For this model to work and be profitable, the buyers need to be pre-qualified so you're not wasting your money.

There can be a lot of expenses in this business. Obviously you have various dues, your MLS fees, lead generation systems, your CRM, lead providers, your marketing, etc. You want to take this into consideration when determining how to hire in the most cost effective manner for your business. If an employee is salaried, you pay all expenses. If an employee works on commission, you typically pay half. It's a good rule of thumb and fairly standard for the industry.

A good place to find buyer's agents is obviously through other agents, brokerages, job websites, employment agencies, colleges and real estate schools—very similar to where you can find the other talent. You should always be proactive in finding talent, so I want you to start today. Always be looking for talent and trying to find your next hire, even if you don't need to hire that person right now or you can't afford to hire that person right now. When the day comes, and it will come because you're following that vision, you will already know who you're going to put in place. It will future pace you to where you want to be, and it will make sure you are continuing to have the mindset of growing your business.

Inside Sales Associate (ISA). Your ISA is a hire that you're going to be thinking about bringing on around the $8-$12 million in production mark. Their job is to get the lead list from the assistant, make the calls, set the appointments, and, last but not least, qualify that appointment. One thing you should expect with an inside sales associate is they are not going to be as good as you at qualifying the appointment, especially if you pay them per appointment. You will have to work out the kinks and teach them how to qualify better, but it will be worth it. It doesn't mean you necessarily stop making prospecting calls. It just means more can be made. Have the ISA sit with you and listen to how you qualify the prospect and set the appointment. Again, lead from the front. It will motivate them to be better.

If you are not at mastery level on the phone, do not hire an ISA; they won't be able to learn from you at the level you need them to, so wait until you are confident that you have it mastered. Hopefully, by the time you get to $10 million in production you have mastered the phone, but keep that in mind before you hire an ISA.

You can expect to pay an ISA between $20,000-$40,000 a year, or between $10-$20 an hour. I don't recommend paying them $10 an hour unless you pay them a bonus on transactions. Paying a bonus can create motivation for the ISA and control your out of pocket costs.

A good place to find your ISA is from other agents. You can also look on job websites like Monster.com, employment agencies, colleges, Craigslist, and real estate schools.

Listing Agent. The last key hire to build your winning team is your listing agent. A listing agent is similar to the buyer's agent, but they focus only on listing properties. They work with sellers instead of buyers. Why do I recommend having a separate buyer's agent and listing agent? Focus. The ways to approach and prepare for each are different, and you want to create experts in particular niches or areas. Having an agent focused solely on listing properties will allow them to better focus on the elements that help secure a listing. Their job is to secure the appointments, conduct the appointments, and secure the listings. You want to ensure the listing agent is negotiating offers when they come in. They also will be responsible for all communication with the seller. Keep in mind the difference between the listing agent and the buyer's agent. The job of the listing agent is to secure an appointment and get a listing whereas the job of a buyer's agent is to sell a home. Sometimes a buyer's agent will be out with the same buyer for several days or weeks showing them homes. For a listing agent, they make the appointment, conduct the appointment, and it's done. Because of this, the pay splits and commissions will be less. You would pay a listing agent between 17% and 30% of the commission. The listing agent could have upwards of three appointments a day, and 17% is extremely profitable. It takes significantly less time and is more predictable to get a listing appointment.

You will want to bring on the listing agent at about the $18- to $20-million mark in production. Prior to hitting that number, you as the leader will typically be on those appointments—that's the best use of your time until that point. As a commissioned listing agent, you will pay half of their expenses. If you choose to put them on salary, then you would be responsible for all their expenses. You can pay a bonus to the listing agent as well, especially if you offer the lower end on commission percentage. The goal is to keep people motivated and give them enough incentive so they want to work hard for you. A great way to find a listing agent is in your office or another brokerage, job websites, colleges, and real estate schools.

KNOW WHO YOU'RE LOOKING FOR

It is important when looking at potential team members to take into consideration the person's personality type. To get a good listing agent, you want to find someone who is direct, dominant, and to the point. These are great qualities for a listing agent and will help them be perceived as an authority with the sellers.

For the buyer's agent, look for those personalities who are influencers. They are the "life of the party" types, are very social, and are great at conversation. They never meet a stranger. These are going to be people who buyers feel comfortable around and who they trust to represent them in the buying process.

Sometimes you will meet somebody and just know they "have it"; they have what it takes to be successful in the real estate business. Oftentimes you can make a dramatic difference in that person's life just by giving them an opportunity. That person is one piece of information away from achieving any level of success they want, just like you.

When you're looking for an administrative assistant, you need to look for someone who is loyal and service oriented. You want someone who is constantly thinking about how to save you time so you can focus on HLAs. Find the right personality with the right experience for each position to build a winning team.

PASS THE BATON; DON'T TOSS BOWLING BALLS

One of the most critical things to remember when you are building your team is to pass the baton; don't toss bowling balls. You want to set your team members up for success, and the way to do that is to teach people what is expected of them, provide them with the tools and systems to execute, and then softly pass the baton to them to run with it.

If you bring in your team members and toss them bowling balls, what it going to happen? They're going to drop them because they weren't expecting it, because it is more than what they are equipped to handle. Help your team win by giving them the proper environment in which to thrive.

Your team will look to you for leadership, and they will model your behavior. Zig Ziglar said it best: "You can have everything in life you want if you will just help enough other people get what they want." I firmly believe this.

Focus on your next step. Hire the right team. Lead from the front. Train for success.

 ACTIONS TO TAKE

1. Begin looking for your next team members now; be prepared for when the right time comes.
2. Early on, bring on the transaction coordinator, because you don't have to pay them until the deal closes.

 KEYS TO SUCCESS

1. Freedom is being able to work on your business and not have to work in your business.
2. Hiring a team is an incremental process based on your production

revenues.

3. You are literally one hire away from becoming as successful as you want to be.

4. One of the most critical things to remember when you are building your team is to pass the baton; don't toss bowling balls.

11. UNLEASH THE POWER OF DIGITAL PRESENTATIONS

What turns me on about the digital age, what excites me personally,
is that you have closed the gap between dreaming and doing.
—BONO

The key word in digital presentations is presentation, and you need to intentionally do more presentations. One of the things that my mentor told me was, "Hoss, always remember you're not making money until you're making money in your sleep." What does that mean? Having tools that work for you when you're not working creates additional revenue streams and allows you to duplicate your efforts. That's a big reason why I focused on listings, because I was making money in my sleep when I had signs in the ground. Digital presentations is another way to be making money when you're not working. Present the content once, record it, and then you can leverage it in many ways and as often as possible. There are several purposes of a digital presentation.

1. **Training and Education.** Provide content and value, and give tools to others. When you educate your buyers, sellers, team members, and other real estate agents, it establishes you as an authority and differentiates you from others.

2. **Meetings and Events.** Conduct digital meetings and events; this includes webinars, chats, live events, and general meetings that need to be more than just a phone call. Leverage the web to conduct seminars for both buyers and sellers. Ensure that the appropriate audiences know what content you have available to them as extended resources.

3. **Virtual Listing Presentations.** Use the digital media option to present to your prospective seller. This can be an efficient and effective way to capture business and get listings.

4. **Virtual Buyer Presentations.** Present opportunities to your buyers through online meetings and appointments. You can present properties to them as well as offer information to them that they need to consider when making a purchase. Anything you would do in person with a buyer can be done online.

5. **Recruiting and Team Building.** It is often difficult to get all your team together in one place, and this is especially true if you have virtual employees. Conduct interviews online with potential

agents or other employees.

When I was an agent, I sold many homes because on the first Monday of every month, I would conduct a home buyer's seminar, and every month I would have a drove of buyers participate as I taught them about the 10 things they needed to avoid in the purchase of their next home. I was the only agent in the entire city that educated the marketplace in this way. It was a big reason that people trusted me and that my repeat referral business was as high as it was. People saw value in me because I gave them value.

> YOU'RE NOT MAKING MONEY UNTIL YOU'RE MAKING MONEY IN YOUR SLEEP.

TYPES OF DIGITAL PRESENTATIONS

What exactly is a digital presentation? Digital presentations can take on multiple formats and be used for a variety of purposes. The best thing about them is that they can be conducted from anywhere. You can be in your office, at your home, in your car, or even on the beach. It doesn't matter where you are—as long as you have Internet access or cell phone reception, you can deliver a digital presentation. You can create them from your smart phone, your tablet, or your computer.

VIDEO

There are various types of video you can produce for your prospects or team. As discussed previously, you need to do a brief video introduction that you send in an email immediately when you receive a new prospect. This helps position you as *different* prior to going to an appointment. I suggest leveraging this tool primarily to deliver a brief personal message to the prospect.

WEBINARS

If you haven't ever conducted a webinar training to a buyer or seller,

I would bet that you have participated in one. In fact, I would bet you attend some type of webinar or digital training on a regular basis. This is an exceptional tool to use with your clients. They are about to make some of the biggest decisions and investments of their lives, and you have the power to educate them on things to take into consideration when buying and selling. Most people would love to have this content available to them and will attend if given the opportunity. Others who don't attend will still appreciate the fact you have the content as validation that you know your stuff and are an expert in your field.

I've conducted over 1,000 webinars, written hundreds of different presentations, authored several books, and delivered countless online presentations. I want to help you learn what I know so you can do the same in your business, because I believe that's where the market is moving towards, and in this digital age, people want to have options. And when you record your presentations and make them available online, someone searching late at night, early morning, or anytime can "experience" what you have to offer if you have digital material available to them online.

It's not enough to just conduct a webinar. To get results from it, you need to have the right ingredients. It is just like a recipe; if any part is missing, it won't come together properly. Make sure you include each component when putting together your presentations.

So you can truly grasp each of the components, I'm going to give you an example of each below.

1. Intro. All you need is a simple introduction to kick off the webinar. "Hey, it's Hoss Pratt. I hope everybody is having a fantastic day today. Before I get started, let's do a quick sound [1]check. Everyone, type in your name and where you're from in the chat box."

2. Bold promise. This needs to be an impact statement to grab the audience's attention. "If you're looking to save tens of thousands of dollars or more on the purchase of your next home, you're in the right spot." Or, "If you're looking for the 5 ways to sell your home the fastest and for the most amount of money, you came to the right place."

3. Hook to end. You always want to hook them to the end to keep them online and engaged. You don't want them to think it's okay to hang up at any time. This is true for every presentation, not just webinars. Remember, it is a one-way communication, and you need to find every way possible to keep them interested. "After this webinar, I'm going to give you a free gift, The 7 Things You Need to Do to Stage Your Home report. I'll show you how to do that in the webinar for everybody that's attending."

4. Command attention. Command their attention, and pull them back in. Give them valid reasons as to why they should listen and pay attention. Tell them, "What I want you to do is pay attention to what you're looking at right now."

5. Qualify yourself. Why should they listen to you? What are your greatest hits? Think of five to 10 one-liners that will show them you are the expert. For example

- Number of years in the business
- Number of clients served
- Special certifications and designations
- Successful stats

6. Future pace. Paint the picture of victory by making them think and see ahead. Help them see clearly what result they are going to get by paying attention to what you have to say. "Once you know these five things, you're going to have the confidence to be able to always go out there and get your property sold in any market condition."

7. Content. On content, you should have anywhere between three and seven topics with each having anywhere between three and six sub-topics beneath each. This is a good rule of thumb and the maximum for a webinar. You want to give enough, but not too much that you lose them.

8. Position the close. This is where you will plant the seed that you are going to be making an offer of some sort at the end of the webinar or presentation. For example, you would say something like, "Here in a few minutes, you're going to have an opportunity to schedule a 10-minute phone call with me where I will show you how to save $10,000 to $20,000 on the purchase of your next home." This gets them thinking toward the offer and if they will take action.

9. Offer. At the end, you're going to close them by making them an offer. It depends on what the goal is on what the offer is going to be, but you will make them an offer. Some offers you may make are

- Book a strategy session or meeting with you
- Download a free report
- Receive a gift or additional offer

Developing successful webinars is key to capitalizing on the digital marketplace. Follow the model and make sure you include all the components to maximize your efforts.

VIRTUAL MEETINGS

Utilizing a virtual meeting platform is another way to communicate and meet with both individuals and groups. Virtual meetings give me, and my staff, the desired freedom I want. By leveraging technology, I am able to communicate with my team as needed anywhere in the world.

Step outside your comfort zone. That feels like turbulence sometimes, but on the other side of turbulence is a smooth ride. Once you use this tool for the first time, you will see that it is as simple as a phone call, but it can have a much bigger impact. There are times when you want it to feel as if you have had a meeting or a presentation instead of just a call. You didn't decide to read this book to be like everybody else. Put yourself out there, and do the things you've never done before. It will change the level of results you achieve, but it will also change your

> STEP OUTSIDE YOUR COMFORT ZONE. THAT FEELS LIKE TURBULENCE SOMETIMES, BUT ON THE OTHER SIDE OF TURBULENCE IS A SMOOTH RIDE.

overall thinking. The more you are willing to do new things, the more innovative you will be naturally.

When trying new technology, don't be afraid to make mistakes. In fact, expect them. People don't expect perfection. I remember the first time I did a webinar. It was a big deal to me. I was asked to do a training for a real estate company. They invited me in and said, "Hoss, we want you to do a webinar. We love what you're doing, and we want our people to hear your training." This was years and years ago when webinars were first coming on the scene. We started the webinar, and there were 1,000 people online and I was as nervous as I could be, knowing I had 1,000 people online listening to me. It was new technology, and I didn't really know how to operate the system. I got through the whole presentation, and I thought, "I killed that; that was awesome." Then I realized I was looking at the area where people can ask questions or make comments. All the comments said variations of, "We can't see your screen." I forgot to hit the Share Screen button at the beginning of the webinar, so the entire presentation was a teleseminar. I had been sitting there going through my entire slide deck while the audience was telling me they couldn't see anything. I couldn't believe it. I thought, "I really screwed up this time."

Making mistakes happens in life a lot. That's okay. Fail forward. What does that mean? It means to learn from the failure to improve going forward. People laughed at Columbus when he said the world was round, and he missed America on his first attempt. The Wright brothers claimed flying was possible and nearly killed themselves trying to prove it, but they failed forward and became the fathers of aviation. Albert Einstein failed his way through academics. Guess what? Failure isn't fatal, and it isn't permanent. Fail forward. Learn from your mistakes and do better next time. Don't hold yourself back out of fear of failure. Take chances and move the needle forward. My motto is "Be bold, take action, and make it happen."

TESTIMONIAL VIDEOS

One thing I do consistently at my events is to have a videographer on hand to capture video testimonials of clients sharing their experience. This is equally effective using your smart phone or a small video recorder. Having and sharing live testimonials from happy customers is an excellent way to capture social proof. Post them on your YouTube page, your website, and all your social media pages.

If you have written testimonials, you can make a video out of them to use on your website or as lead ins to your presentations. Take the words and have them scroll in on slides and set the presentation to music. This is effective as well and is a great way to utilize written testimonials in an interactive way. An additional tip is to transcribe your video testimonials into written form so you have both written and video testimonials.

WEBSITE

Having a website is expected as a minimum if you are a real estate agent today. Most agents only set their sites up to showcase listings and allow buyers to search for properties. To stand apart, use your arsenal to showcase your expertise. Post educational and testimonial videos. Have things of value available beyond what is expected.

SOCIAL MEDIA

Utilize social media to communicate a variety of things. Post new listings, properties sold, new testimonials (whether written or video), live video tips for the day, inspirational messages, content of value for buyers and sellers, and even cartoons or jokes. Build your following by offering something for signing up or liking your page—it can just be something downloadable. It is important to stay in front of your prospects and clients on a regular basis, and social media is an easy way to make that happen.

EMAIL

We all use email dozens of times a day. Use today's technology with your emails to include images, video clips, links, and other items of value to your prospects and customers. Create content (or outsource someone to write it for you) that is engaging and has good calls to action to get people to do what you want them to do.

BUILD YOUR CONTENT

You previously identified your specific niche markets, and I have shared numerous ways throughout the book to become an expert. In order to maximize your digital presence, you next need to create content based on your niches and areas of expertise. Your content communicates your solution while at the same time pounding their pain. Everything is dialed in for your copy and your message, because the content is what ascends you and makes you the expert in their eyes. It is crucial your content be strategically thought out to provide value and solutions to your audience.

There is an endless amount of content possibilities. To build successful content that ties back to you, you can utilize my model:

DIGITAL PRESENTATION CONTENT DEVELOPMENT MODEL
   Item
   1. Define your niche.
   2. Be an expert.
   3. Identify the pain.
   4. Develop a solution.
   5. Produce content.
   6. Present content.
   7. Distribute the content.

Note that sometimes the content is vast and comprehensive; other times, the content is a single subject that you just want to share some tips and tools with the audience. Whatever you want to accomplish, the model is still valid. Follow the model, and you will be successful in building an arsenal of digital presentations.

CONNECTING WITH YOUR AUDIENCE

One of the biggest benefits to digital presentation is connecting with your audience. When people can see you and hear you, you are more real to them. Make sure you have good energy, because it is often only a one-way communication. You have to be the engagement and enthusiasm for both sides.

Also know that when you are presenting a webinar especially, people are often multitasking on the other side. Be compelling and engaging, and make sure your content has value to the audience to keep their attention. Did you know that some meeting platforms have an attentiveness rating that can tell when you're not paying attention or if you have minimized your screen and are working on something else? I use the attentiveness rating to help me know how to better control the audience. It gives me a pulse of whether or not I'm presenting the right content the right way to keep their attention. If I see the attentiveness rating going down, I ask for specific engagement. I tell them what's coming up is important or I ask them to write something down to bring their attention back to me.

BE INTERESTING AND SHARE INFORMATION OF VALUE IN VARIOUS WAYS THAT KEEPS PEOPLE ENGAGED.

There are various ways to keep the audience's attention. One way, as I stated above, it to make sure your energy level is high. You also want to engage the audience. A great way to do this is by asking questions. People want you to be interesting. Change up the way you present to keep their engagement—most people in today's digital age have the attention span of a flea. Use different presentation methods to deliver your message. Show your face, use slides, share trivia, ask questions, have them write things down, tell stories and present case studies, and give third-party validation where possible. Changing up your presentation will get better engagement and appeal to various personality styles. Remember when we talked about the DISC personality styles earlier in the book? Each style likes to be presented to differently. Make sure you are not only presenting in your preferred style. Mix it up. Be interesting and share information of value in various ways that keeps people engaged.

Whether you are building a mega team so you can scale your business or you are building a lifestyle business, being innovative is equally important. There is no right or wrong on the type of business you want to build, but there are definitely different levels of success you can achieve, and that success is determined by the things you are willing to do that others are not that set you apart from your competition. Utilizing technology is one way to set yourself apart. No matter which type of business you are building, you still need to be perceived as an expert.

OTHER DIGITAL TOOLS

In order to get the true benefit of your digital arsenal, you need to have things automated. You need to have an automated scheduler. If someone wants to make an appointment with me, I send them to my scheduler. Then they can match up their schedule with mine, and I don't spent any of my time doing that.

If you aren't already using one, you need to get a service that allows you to sign contracts and agreements online. Make it easy for people to do business with you. If they have to print out documents, sign them, and get them back to you, chances are the process will be delayed.

THE MORE DIGITAL YOUR FOOTPRINT, THE MORE YOU ARE ACCEPTED AS AN EXPERT.

Let me close this by saying that utilizing the power of digital presentations is essential in this era of real estate marketing. The more digital your footprint, the more you are accepted as the leading authority and a local expert. Having all of the things listed above will be expected-just like having a website is now expected. Be ahead of the game, and continue to innovate as technology changes. Utilize it to give yourself more breadth. Give yourself every opportunity to shine and show your expertise through the use of technology. If you don't, your competitors will.

Remember, digital means freedom. Virtual presentations allow you to work anywhere in the world, reach more people, provide more value, increase efficiency, and maximize effectiveness.

☞ ACTIONS TO TAKE

1. Build a digital arsenal relating to your niches.
2. Start getting client testimonials, both written and video.
3. Utilize the power of digital presentations to expand your opportunities and growth.

KEYS TO SUCCESS

1. You're not making money until you're making money in your sleep. Digital presentations can work for you when you're not working.
2. Make sure you include these components when creating a webinar: intro, bold promise, hook to the end, command attention, qualify yourself, future pace, content, position to close, and the offer.
3. Step outside your comfort zone. That feels like turbulence sometimes, but on the other side of turbulence is a smooth ride.
4. When trying new technology, don't be afraid to make mistakes. In fact, expect them. People don't expect perfection.
5. One of the biggest benefits to digital presentation is connecting with your audience. When people can see you and hear you, you are more real to them.
6. Make sure you are not only presenting in your preferred style. Mix it up. Be interesting and share information of value in various ways that maintain engagement.
7. Utilizing the power of digital presentation is essential in this era of real estate marketing. The more digital your footprint, the more you are accepted as contemporary, up-to-date, and an expert.
8. Digital means freedom.

12. Take Action and Make It Happen

The path to success is to take massive, determined action.
—Tony Robbins

Knowledge is worth nothing if it isn't put to use. Because you have invested your time in this book, I know that you want to take your business to a higher level. As a result of this book, I hope you have moved outside your traditional box and created bigger dreams than you previously thought were possible. Now it's time to start achieving those dreams. To create legendary success, it's going to take massive action.

Remember, one of the biggest things you need to continue doing to create greater and greater success is to continue to invest in yourself. This will keep you fresh, motivated, and inspired. No matter what level of success you achieve, there's always another level. The higher levels that you achieve will bring you greater freedom with your time and your money. With this freedom, a whole new world of choices and opportunities will open up to you. Before I conclude, I want to reiterate some ongoing ways to invest in yourself.

THE HIGHER LEVELS THAT YOU ACHIEVE WILL BRING YOU GREATER FREEDOM WITH YOUR TIME AND YOUR MONEY.

SURROUND YOURSELF WITH SUCCESS

I spend thousands and thousands of dollars every year investing in myself so I continue to grow my success year after year. How do I spend those dollars?

- Coaches
- Mentors
- Masterminds
- Books, courses, and products
- Events and conferences

I saturate myself with intelligence and ideas that others have used to grow their businesses and reach their goals. These things make me a better person in all areas of my life, not just business. I've made many references to Tony Robbins throughout this book, as he is one of those handful of people who have had a tremendous impact on me. Tony has a great quote to bring this home: "If you want to be successful, find someone who has achieved the results you want, copy what they do, and you'll achieve the same results." You don't need to reinvent the wheel. Just find others you admire who have had the level of success that you want, and duplicate it. Proven success is what I've been sharing with you in these pages. It's now up to you to continue the process and surround yourself with people and things that will complement your business.

COACHES

Coaches are people who are expert in helping you get where you want to go. They are paid advisors. If you don't have a coach, you need to get one. They will help guide you strategically, push you to achieve more, and hold you accountable to yourself. They have their eyes on the big picture and will steer you toward greater results. I still utilize a success coach, because you've never achieved too much to outgrow having one. Having a coach also helps me be a better coach. How many professional athletes do you know who no longer have a coach? None. Why do people hire me as their coach? Because I've achieved the results they want, and I give them the models that will get them to the next level.

MENTORS

Mentors are people in your life who have life and/or business experiences to share and choose to invest their time with you. Mentors are unpaid advisors. I've shared with you about what a significant impact my mentor (Jimbo) had on helping me get into the real estate business and creating my initial success. It is not uncommon to have several mentors in your life who each cover different things—spirituality, relationships, personal life, business, and more. Don't act like you know it all; take advantage of those who have wisdom and experience over you. You can create a significant advantage by utilizing those people in your life who have gone before you and already lived the trials and challenges you now face. A mentor is someone you look up to and who you feel you can work well with from a personality standpoint. You want a mentor who is successful and who seems genuinely happy with their life and career. Your mentors need to be able to both inspire and motivate you to take action.

MASTERMINDS

Masterminds are groups made up of those other five-percenters like you who are willing to come together and share ideas, best practices, and successes. Sometimes these groups are brought together by an industry expert to facilitate the group, and other times the groups are put together and led by the individual members. The key to success in engaging in masterminds is to truly bring together others with different levels of success and growth so each person can contribute to the others' growth.

BOOKS, COURSES, AND PRODUCTS

You are already a believer in books as a source of knowledge as evidenced by the fact you purchased the *Listing Boss*. With today's technology, there is a plethora of ways to get intelligence. There are trade journals, YouTube, books, tapes, videos, tools, and other resources readily available to anyone seeking them. The *Listing Boss* was originally developed as an online course that I condensed down in these pages. The great thing about most of these options is that you can explore them any time, day or night. They aren't dependent on anyone else's participation, so you can fit them into your schedule easily.

CONFERENCES AND EVENTS

There are lots of reasons to invest in conferences and events. I attend many throughout the year because they are inspiring, and the synergies of the events motivate me to take action. People who attend my conferences, who are often my coaching clients, tell me that going through things at an experiential level just brings it all home for them and gives a completely different perspective. It's like the difference between learning about skiing by watching an instructional video versus actually being taught by an instructor and skiing down a mountain slope; which do you think will give you the better perspective on how to ski?

BUY SPEED

It's that simple—buy speed. Life is fast, and sometimes short cutting the time to learn and absorb something can add thousands of dollars to your bottom line in dramatically less time by "buying speed." Just a few months ago, I wanted to learn Evernote. Evernote is a cross-platform app designed for note taking, organizing, and archiving. The app allows users to create a "note" which can be a piece of formatted text, a full webpage, a photograph, a voice memo, or a handwritten note. Notes can also have file attachments.

I knew Evernote was a complex beast in a lot of ways, with multiple capabilities. Like I always do when I want to master something, I googled "best Evernote coach and consultant," and I found a list that I narrowed down from 10 to three. I interviewed the top three, and I found the top Evernote expert in the entire world. This lady is amazing. I called her office and hired her to give me one month of coaching to show me and my team everything that she knew in Evernote so we could become fast experts. The learning curve and time spent would have been much more than the investment I made in coaching. I bought speed. That's always the answer.

IF YOU WANT TO BECOME AN EXPERT AT SOMETHING FAST, BUY SPEED.

All of those things above we talked about to surround yourself with success can be used to buy speed. The faster and more comprehensively you want to learn something, the more it typically costs. Determine the value to you and your team, and don't hesitate to buy speed to increase and grow your business.

Think outside the box. Remember, "For things to change, you must change; change your thinking, change your results."

BURN THE BOATS

I want to close out this book with a story that changed my life. I've shared it in a lot of my seminars, because it has had such a big impact on me. The story is called "Burn the Boats."

In 1519, a man named Hernando Cortés set sail on a voyage that would take him from the shores of Cuba to the Yucatán Peninsula. He had 500 soldiers, 100 sailors, and 16 horses on 11 ships. They were going to capture the world's richest treasure. This was a treasure of gold, silver, and jewels that had been held by the same army for over 600 years! Everybody knew about this treasure, because army after army had attempted to conquer this treasure before. Army after army failed when they tried to take the treasure.

Cortés knew that he had to have a different approach if he wanted a different outcome. Cortés was a smart guy, and he was not going to go in and just start fighting like everyone else had already done! Cortés knew that he had to have an army of people whose commitment was beyond that which an ordinary person considered normal. Rather than just sign people up for the mission, Cortés laid out his vision. He laid out the vision for his men. He shared with them what their lives would be like when they grew in wealth and in favor by capturing the treasure. He gave every person a vision of legendary success. Then they were on their way.

Halfway thru the voyage, Cortés realized he had a problem. All his men who were so certain of capturing the treasure before they left on their voyage became less certain. In fact, they turned into whiners. They said things like, "Mr. Cortés, please turn this ship around. I'm getting queasy; this doesn't seem right." They started having second thoughts, and when they got there, they didn't just walk in and fight! They pulled their ships up to the shore, and they waited on the beach.

As they waited, Cortés gathered everybody around and had talks with them. They talked about what their treasure was going to be like, what their children were going to grow up like with this wealth, and how their children were going to grow up in a much better environment than they did. He painted this picture again, and the men were reminded of their vision.

The day came when it was time to go in and take this treasure. Cortés didn't go in and start fighting. He gathered his men around, and he said three words that would change everything. Can you think of three words that could literally alter the course of your life? He leaned in and said to the men, "Burn the boats." And they did! They torched their boats! Why? Because with their boats burned, they had no choice but to win! They burned Plan B, which left them with only one option—make Plan A work.

Cortés and his men burned their own boats, went in, and took the treasure. They won. The same army had held the treasure for over 600 years, and they captured it from them. Why? They had no choice! They had no out. They had no excuses. Therefore, they had to figure out a way to succeed.

My question to you is, "What are your boats? What's getting in your way of success?" Get rid of Plan B, go out there, and be all in! Be committed just like Hernando Cortés and his army were at achieving success. Be committed to change, and follow the exact action plan you need to follow to get where you want to be. Own it. You control your destiny, nobody else.

Somebody said the biggest fear is realizing how powerful we are as humans and that there is no end to our individual potential. You really can become anything you want, but you can't play it safe. You only have one life. Make it legendary. Burn the boats!

> YOU ONLY HAVE ONE LIFE. MAKE IT LEGENDARY.

 ACTIONS TO TAKE

1. Commit to your success.
2. Figure out what your boats are, and burn them.
3. Take massive action.

KEYS TO SUCCESS

1. Knowledge is worth nothing if it isn't put to use.
2. The higher levels that you achieve will bring you greater freedom with your time and your money.
3. If you want to be successful, find someone who has achieved the results you want, copy what they do, and you'll achieve the same results.
4. If you want to become an expert at something fast, buy speed.
5. You really can become anything you want, but you can't play it safe.
6. You only have one life. Make it legendary.
7. Burn the boats.
8. Join **Listing Boss Academy**. See my invitation on page 201.

About the Author

One word describes the man who gets more results out of real estate brokers and agents than any other trainer in the country ... *passion*.

A nationally known authority when it comes to lead generation and lead conversion, Hoss Pratt has demonstrated time and time again during his stellar career that using his revolutionary strategies can move brokers and agents from stuck to super charged in just months—changing lives and changing fortunes. He is a master at converting prospects into clients and fence-sitters into sellers.

What separates Hoss from all other coaches, real estate trainers, and so-called gurus is his ability to get results FAST. He's presented over 1,100 sold-out webinars and online events, conducted over 1,300 live seminars in 48 states, knocked on over 100,000 doors, made over 200,000 prospecting/sales calls, presented at over 2,100 kitchen tables, and has amassed over 5,500 hours personally coaching thousands of successful agents and industry professionals.

Hoss is also an in-demand keynote presenter and trainer at major real estate conventions and live events, where he shares the stage with other nationally recognized industry leaders.

Nothing is more important to Hoss than his family. He takes every opportunity to spend the majority of his time with the love of his life, wife, and best friend, Mykanna, and their three daughters, Kennedy, Piper, and Ivy.

Bonus Content - Building a Business Plan

One of the most important pieces to success is having a solid plan in place. It is my sincere desire to give you the tools you need in order to get the results you want. That is why I'm providing you with this bonus content. If you already have a business plan in place, you are ahead of the game. If you don't, I've provided a model for you here to get you started.

I encourage you to complete this plan as the next step in your journey. This plan is all about you and your goals. If you follow the plan as you design it, you will see a level of results greater than you've previously seen.

PURPOSE

The purpose of this plan is to provide a specific and clear guideline of set goals for the next 12 months. This plan is a one-year, month-to-month plan designed to achieve my personal annual financial goal (Gross Income to me) of $_____.

The plan is specific as to the amount of business-generating activities and to the types of these activities I will need to accomplish each week, each month, and each quarter of the year.

I am committed to monitoring my business generation activities each thirty days in order to make sure that I am on target. I am willing to alter my activities and my plan if it is not working for me. I am committed to learning and practicing new skills and habits that will help me achieve my goals.

This plan is designed to create growth for me, both financially and personally. By signing this document I am committing my efforts and energies toward the accomplishment of this plan.

_____   _____

Signature   Date

OBJECTIVES FOR
THE NEXT YEAR

The following are the major objectives that I want to accomplish during the next year (gross commission income, prospecting contacts, listings taken, listings sold, buyer sales, education & training, travel, purchases, health, personal, etc.):

1. _____

_____

2. _____

_____

3. _____

_____

4. _____

_____

5. _____

_____

6. _____

_____

7. _____

_____

8. _____

_____

9. _____

_____

10. _____

_____

ANALYSIS

In the last 12 Months, I have accomplished the following numbers. I will use these numbers in realistically setting my goals for the next 12 Months.

1. My (GCI) over the last 12 months was $_____.

2. I worked an average of _____ hours per week during the _____ weeks that I worked this past year.

3. My average sales price was $_____.

4. I took _____ listings.

5. I had _____ of those listings sell (close).

6. I averaged _____ hours per week of active lead generation.

7. My three most productive sources for listings were:

   1. _____

   2. _____

   3. _____

8. My three most productive sources for buyers were:

   1. _____

2. _____

3. _____

9. My total number of units closed was: _____.

10. My average commission per closed side was $_____.

FINANCIAL AND PRODUCTION GOALS

1. My closed commission (GCI) goal _____

2. My average commission per side (unit) will be _____

3. The number of closed sales (sides) necessary to achieve my income goal (#1 divided by #2) _____

4. My projected closings will come from
    A. Listings Sold _____
    B. Buyers Sold _____

5. Projecting that % of my listings will sell, the number of listings I will need to take will be (#4A divided by the % of #5)

    _____

6. Considering that % of my buyer contracts will cancel, I will need to write a total number of (#4B divided by (100% minus the % of #6) _____

7. Since I plan to get listings on % of my listing appointments, I will need to go on the following number of listing appointments (#5 divided by the % of #7) _____

8. Since I sell a home to % of the buyers I work with, I will need to work with the following number of new buyers (#6 divided by the % of #8) _____

9. The number of appointments I need to set this year:
    Listing Appointments _____ Per Month _____ Per Week

    New Buyers _____ Per Month _____ Per Week

    Total _____ Per Month _____ Per Week

BUSINESS GENERATION ACTION PLAN

I know that business generation (prospecting and lead management) is one of the most important activities in building production, income, and long-term business success. Therefore, the final part of my business plan is focus on, and commit to the prospecting I will do this year.

While I cannot always control the results, I know that I can manage my time and activities. The more time I spend marketing my services, the more likely it is that I will achieve my goals. Therefore, I commit to the following business generation action plan:

Prospecting Activity   **Weekly Hours**   **Monthly Hours**

1. _____   _____   _____

2. _____   _____   _____

3. _____   _____   _____

4. _____   _____   _____

Total Hours: _____   _____

Invitation to Join

LISTING BOSS ACADEMY

with Hoss Pratt

A real estate solution positioning you to dominate your market

From the Desk of Hoss Pratt

—

Invitation to Join
Listing Boss Academy

A real estate solution positioning you to dominate your market

I want to congratulate you for completing the journey of reading *Listing Boss*. I have no doubt that what you take from this book will impact you and your business for years to come. However, you may be sitting there wondering what's next? Where do I go from here? How do I implement everything laid out in this book the fastest most efficient and effective way possible? How do I get results that I've never achieved before? How do I quickly grow my business with certainty? How do I navigate the challenging waters of entrepreneurship and business building?

I've got great news for you. I never intended your journey to stop at this book. In fact, I look at this as the beginning of our journey. A journey that's going to be extremely valuable for the trajectory of your business. That's the reason I created Listing Boss Academy. An elite program designed to make any real estate agent extraordinarily successful in less than 12-months.

Listing Boss Academy is a revolutionary coaching and implementation program that focuses on the four pillars of success in real estate...Mindset, Marketing, Systems, and Conversion. Listing Boss Academy goes deep into each of the pillars by implementing the core foundations to ensure long-lasting success.

I developed Listing Boss Academy to teach you the *ultimate* approach to dominate your market and make your competition irrelevant. Here's where it gets good... The agents that complete the academy generate an average of $1 million in additional gross closings each month. In many cases, this translates to $15K-$30K in additional revenue. Those are HUGE numbers that will inevitably change your life. I want you to create this kind of growth in perpetuity.

I want to personally invite you to continue this journey together and join Listing Boss Academy.

Become a member of *Listing Boss Academy* and you will -----

- Gain access to my proprietary systems and marketing programs that get results fast

- Differentiate yourself from your competition so you're the clear choice for any prospect

- Know the exact process to generate 5 to 30 listings a month every single month

- Attract leads ready to sell by delivering an effective value proposition

- Build the foundation to produce an additional one million dollars in closings each month

- See an immediate change in 90 DAYS ----- that's our standard.

Working hard and working smart are not the same thing. Time and effort have little to do with making money. In Listing Boss Academy you're going to learn how to only spend your time and energy on the actions that drive revenue to your business.

This isn't just a system for beginners trying to find their place in real estate. Listing Boss Academy is a comprehensive system for all agents who are driven to win. As a part of this community, you will be able to engage with and learn from your peers' experiences as well as my own. You'll learn practical methods from me, your coach, to position yourself as the strongest, fiercest competitor in your market.

You'll learn how to -----

- Build a digital marketing machine that makes money while you sleep

- Develop a method of operations that focuses you on high-value actions daily

- Become the undisputed expert in your niche

- Market yourself as the recognized authority in your field

- Learn to attract prospects you want with targeted marketing

- Be more organized and employ action plans to automate your business

- Enhance your value proposition with any seller objection

- Create campaigns effortlessly with fill-in-the-blank templates

- Integrate new technology easily to enhance your sales, not complicate them

Over the last decade, I've helped thousands of agents generate millions of dollars in commissions by following my proven systems. Listing Boss Academy is specifically designed to take you from where you are now to the next level. If you're a new agent it's designed to take you to six figures. If you're already in the business it's designed to double your business year after year. In Listing Boss Academy you're going to get access to the best of the best systems, marketing, tools, scripts, resources, and strategies to find the best opportunities in your market in real time.

My passion is helping agents get to the next level, create more commissions and to do so in less time because if you don't have a system that runs your business then you'll be a statistic. In fact, 95% of the transactions are done by 5% of the agents in almost every market. My goal is to help you become a 5%er because that's where freedom exists. And I believe the missing link for those who struggle... is not having systems.

The reason most agents are flying by the seat of their pants, jack of all trades master of none, throwing spaghetti at the wall to see what sticks, is because they don't have systems in their business, and that's the reason I created Listing Boss Academy to fix this problem once and for all. If this colossal problem is not fixed, no agent will get to the next level.

As I take you on this journey you're going to build an asset — a business that runs like a well-oiled machine — that can grow as high as you want. Not only that but you're going to be a part of a community of people that are success-minded growth thinkers just like you.

You're going to get everything you need to grow your business in Listing Boss Academy. I want you to imagine having the ability to double your business in 12- months. How would that change your life? Imagine having complete certainty of where your next closing is going to come from, the certainty of knowing what you need to do every single day to drive results for your business. Listing Boss Academy will allow you to build a rock solid business on a firm foundation.

So please accept my invitation to Listing Boss Academy. This is the one investment that will change everything for you. And I don't care what you've tried in the past, what you've tried that hasn't worked, you've never experienced a solution like Listing Boss Academy. So join the family, take action now, and make the investment for yourself, for your business, for your life.

Dominate your market. Close more sales than ever.
Become a LISTING BOSS.

Go to www.ListingBossAcademy.com to join today.

Sincerely,

Hoss Pratt

CONTACT US

Hoss Pratt International, Inc.
6009 W. Parker Rd., #149-230
Plano, TX 75093
Phone: 1.800.683.HOSS (4677)
Email: results@hosspratt.com

FOLLOW US

Linked in.
www.LinkedIn.com/in/hosspratt

www.facebook.com/HossPratt/

www.twitter.com/hosspratt

You Tube
www.youtube.com/c/HossPratt

Instagram
www.Instragram.com/hosspratt

NOTES

NOTES